AMERICAN ★ HISTORY

The HARLEM RENAISSANCE

An African American Cultural Movement

By Tamra B. Orr

Portions of this book originally appeared in
The Harlem Renaissance by Stuart A. Kallen.

LUCENT
PRESS

Published in 2019 by
Lucent Press, an Imprint of Greenhaven Publishing, LLC
353 3rd Avenue
Suite 255
New York, NY 10010

Designer: Deanna Paternostro
Editor: Jessica Moore

Cataloging-in-Publication Data

Names: Orr, Tamra B.
Title: The Harlem Renaissance: An African American Cultural Movement / Tamra B. Orr.
Description: New York : Lucent Press, 2019. | Series: American history | Includes index.
Identifiers: ISBN 9781534564237 (pbk.) | ISBN 9781534564213 (library bound) | ISBN 9781534564220 (ebook)
Subjects: LCSH: Harlem Renaissance--Juvenile literature. | African Americans--History--1877-1964--Juvenile literature. | African American arts--20th century--Juvenile literature. | Harlem (New York, N.Y.)--Intellectual life--20th century--Juvenile literature. | New York (N.Y.)--Intellectual life--20th century--Juvenile literature.
Classification: LCC E185.6 O76 2019 | DDC 305.896'0730747--dc23
Printed in the United States of America

CPSIA compliance information: Batch #BS18KL: For further information contact Greenhaven Publishing LLC, New York, New York at 1-844-317-7404.

Please visit our website, www.greenhavenpublishing.com. For a free color catalog of all our high-quality books, call toll free 1-844-317-7404 or fax 1-844-317-7405.

Contents

Foreword

The United States is a relatively young country. It has existed as its own nation for more than 200 years, but compared to nations such as China that have existed since ancient times, it is still in its infancy. However, the United States has grown and accomplished much since its birth in 1776. What started as a loose confederation of former British colonies has grown into a major world power whose influence is felt around the globe.

How did the United States manage to develop into a global superpower in such a short time? The answer lies in a close study of its unique history. The story of America is unlike any other—filled with colorful characters, a variety of exciting settings, and events too incredible to be anything other than true.

Too often, the experience of history is lost among the basic facts: names, dates, places, laws, treaties, and battles. These fill countless textbooks, but they are rarely compelling on their own. Far more interesting are the stories that surround those

basic facts. It is in discovering those stories that students are able to see history as a subject filled with life—and a subject that says as much about the present as it does about the past.

The titles in this series allow readers to immerse themselves in the action at pivotal historical moments. They also encourage readers to discuss complex issues in American history—many of which still affect Americans today. These include racism, states' rights, civil liberties, and many other topics that are in the news today but have their roots in the earliest days of America. As such, readers are encouraged to think critically about history and current events.

Each title is filled with excellent tools for research and analysis. Fully cited quotations from historical figures, letters, speeches, and documents provide students with firsthand accounts of major events. Primary sources bring authority to the text, as well. Sidebars highlight these quotes and primary sources, as well as interesting figures and events. Annotated bibliographies allow students to locate and evaluate sources for further information on the subject.

A deep understanding of America's past is necessary to understand its present and its future. Sometimes you have to look back in order to see how to best move forward, and that is certainly true when writing the next chapter in the American story.

1909
The National
Association for
the Advancement
of Colored People
(NAACP) is founded.

1917
Marcus Garvey moves to
Harlem and founds the
United Negro Improvement
Association (UNIA).

1920
Eugene O'Neill's play
The Emperor Jones
debuts in November.

1909	1913–1919	1917	1919	1920	1920s

1919
Race riots explode in
cities throughout the
country, creating the
"Red Summer of Hate."

1920s
Huge numbers of black
Americans leave New
York to travel abroad.

1913–1919
Early jazz is first heard
in New York City.

A Timeline

1921
Shuffle Along opens on Broadway in New York City.

1935
The Works Progress Administration (WPA) begins providing government-sponsored jobs to many Harlem-based artists and writers. The Harlem Race Riot is sparked by anger over racial discrimination.

1926
Harlem's Savoy Ballroom opens.

1921   **1923**   **1926**   **1929**   **1935**

1923
Duke Ellington and his band arrive in New York. The legendary Cotton Club opens in Harlem.

1929
The Great Depression begins.

A GREAT AWAKENING

Many cultures have experienced a "golden age"—a time when culture and people thrived. Writers created great literature; artists made masterpieces; songwriters created music that defined their generation; and actors delighted audiences on the stage. Readers, listeners, and crowds absorbed the richness of these moments and shared them. People were enlightened, or awakened.

For many black Americans, that golden age arrived in the 1920s. Harlem, a neighborhood in New York City, was the focal point of this cultural awakening. Hundreds of thousands of black American workers headed north—many to Harlem.

Between 1918 and the mid-1930s, the neighborhood thrived as a centerpiece for black American culture and the movement known as the Harlem Renaissance. Renaissance was an old French word that meant "rebirth," so it felt like the perfect title for the changes many black Americans were experiencing. The movement was primarily led by African American writers, playwrights, actors, singers, artists, and jazz and blues musicians. They came from many backgrounds but did not necessarily share the same beliefs about art, politics, or society. However, they all shared a common goal. They wanted to provide a unifying voice for the 10 million black Americans trying to coexist with the 80 million white people living in the United States at that time.

A Struggle for Equality

The Harlem Renaissance began as World War I ended in 1918 and tapered off in the 1930s. However, the movement's impact lingered for several decades.

In large part, the Harlem Renaissance resulted from the ongoing struggle black Americans had with extreme poverty, racism, segregation, and

African Americans faced segregation in many cities throughout the country.

violence in nearly every American city and state.

Black Americans were prevented from finding good jobs, buying homes, and attending decent schools. Many lived in segregated neighborhoods where they patronized black-owned restaurants, theaters, clothing shops, and taverns. Black Americans were commonly prohibited from using public spaces, including swimming pools, parks, and restrooms.

Life was particularly difficult for black Americans living in the South and in rural areas of the Midwest. The racist group the Ku Klux Klan (KKK) was a powerful social and political force in many states.

Mayors, police chiefs, and even state legislators and governors were among its millions of members. The KKK terrorized black communities and lynched (to kill someone by mob action for an alleged crime) countless black Americans to prevent them from exercising their civil rights.

This terrorism, coupled with poor economic conditions and race riots in many cities, led many black southerners to uproot their lives. In what is called the Great Migration, millions of African Americans moved to industrial cities in the North, such as New York City, where there was a greater degree of freedom and opportunity.

A Mythical City

Working-class black Americans brought their unique culture to their new urban settings. Notable black American contributions to society included blues and jazz music, which first emerged in New Orleans, Louisiana, before traveling up the Mississippi River and spreading east to Chicago, Illinois, and New York City. In the world of literature, authors such as Paul Laurence Dunbar, whose parents had been slaves, achieved fame writing about life in the poetic dialect of southern African Americans. Dunbar's 1902 book, *The Sport of the Gods*, was the first novel about black life in New York City. In it, Dunbar described the mythical status the city held in the imaginations of black southerners:

They had heard of New York as a place vague and far away, a city that, like Heaven, to them had existed by faith alone. All the days of their lives they had heard about it, and it seemed to them the centre of all the glory, all the wealth, and all the freedom of the world.[1]

While getting a job was possible for many black Americans, many employment options were low paying and considered by some to be low status.

Like some European immigrants, who may had heard rumors that New York's streets were paved with gold, the reality of the city may have disappointed some African Americans. Unskilled black women living in Harlem labored as maids, dressmakers, beauticians, and cooks. Men were hired as elevator operators, shoe shiners, porters, doormen, messengers, waiters, janitors, and day laborers. However, even these jobs presented better opportunities than those in the South. Additionally, unlike most of the South, Harlem had many black-owned shops and restaurants, as well as black professionals, including lawyers, doctors, nurses, teachers, and preachers.

A Thin Veil

While a few black business owners, landlords, and artists were financially successful, many Harlem residents remained poor before, during, and after the renaissance. However, the mix of old and new cultures from the South, New York City, and even the Caribbean provided artistic inspiration for those leading the Harlem Renaissance. As history professor Cary D. Wintz wrote in *Black Culture and the Harlem Renaissance,*

> [The neighborhood] provided the material and the setting for many literary creations of the Renaissance. The poetry, short stories, and novels of the period abound with scenes and characters lifted from Harlem's streets and cabarets … Harlem though … was a teeming, overcrowded ghetto, and much of its laughter and gaiety only thinly veiled the misery and poverty that was becoming the standard of life for the new black urban masses. This, too, was reflected by the Harlem Renaissance.[2]

What made the era so unique was the fact that it was not only black people celebrating their culture in what was called the the "World's Greatest Negro Metropolis." White Americans were also learning about the joys, troubles, successes, and degradations of life for African Americans.

The Harlem Renaissance was one of the first times that black and white Americans read the same literature, attended theater together, danced together, and sang together. It was a brief period, however, and racism was still rampant among many white Americans. However, for those in New York City's black communities, the renaissance proved to be a celebration of pride, culture, identity, and history. For the first time, the achievements of black Americans were visible for all to see—and after three centuries of racism, enslavement, and prejudice, black Americans ceased being invisible.

Chapter One

A CHANGING URBAN CULTURE

Harlem covers around 3 square miles (7.77 sq km) of Manhattan Island in the northern, or uptown, area of New York City. The neighborhood's original borders were 125th Street to the South, 155th Street to the North, Morningside Drive on the West, and the East and Harlem Rivers on the East.

In the early 1900s, Harlem was home to more than 150,000 black people who represented a melting pot of African Americans from around the United States as well as immigrants from African countries, Jamaica, Haiti, Cuba, and Puerto Rico. In 1925, Harlem had only been the center of black urban culture for about 15 years. How it transformed into the "World's Greatest Negro Metropolis" can be traced to a combination of capitalism, poverty, opportunity, and racism.

Historian Leon Litwack described the early decades of the 20th century as "the most violent and repressive period in the history of race relations in the United States."[3] This was especially true in Virginia, Louisiana, Alabama, Mississippi, Georgia, and the Carolinas, where 80 percent of black Americans lived in rural areas as sharecroppers, which means they farmed land owned by others for a small percentage of the crops. Sharecroppers were the poorest of the poor, often working long hours, living in bad conditions, and suffering from malnutrition and ill health.

Between 1910 and 1930, about 1.5 million black southerners had had enough. They left behind terrible conditions in the South and moved north, settling in cities such as Chicago; Detroit, Michigan; Cleveland, Ohio; and Philadelphia, Pennsylvania. The Great

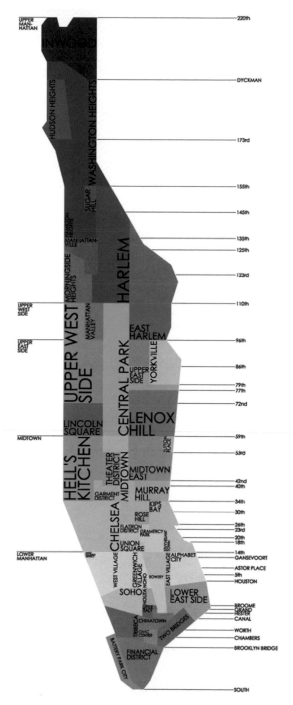

While the names and borders of many of Manhattan's neighborhoods have remained unchanged for more than a century, the constant arrival of new residents from across the country and around the world has transformed many areas of New York City.

The Great Migration completely changed Harlem and resulted in many families moving into the area. Shown here is a photo of families in Harlem in the 1920s.

Nothing Like It

Author, educator, and early civil rights activist James Weldon Johnson was one of the leading literary voices of the Harlem Renaissance. Writing for *Survey Graphic* magazine in March 1925, Johnson described Harlem:

> In the make-up of New York, Harlem is not merely a Negro colony or community, it is a city within a city, the greatest Negro city in the world. It is not a slum or a fringe, it is located in the heart of Manhattan and occupies one of the most beautiful and healthful sections of the city. It is not a "quarter" of dilapidated tenements, but is made up of [new] apartments and handsome dwellings, with well-paved and well-lighted streets. It has its own churches, social and civic centers, shops, theatres and other places of amusement. And it contains more Negroes to the square mile than any other spot on earth. A stranger who rides up magnificent Seventh Avenue on a bus or in an automobile must be struck with surprise at the transformation which takes place after he crosses One Hundred and Twenty-fifth Street. Beginning there, the population suddenly darkens and he rides through twenty-five solid blocks where the passers-by, the shoppers, those sitting in restaurants, coming out of theatres, standing in doorways and looking out of windows are practically all Negroes … There is nothing just like it in any other city in the country, for there is no preparation for it; no change in the character of the houses and streets; no change, indeed, in the appearance of the people, except their color.[1]

1. James Weldon Johnson, "The Making of Harlem," *Survey Graphic*, March 1925, etext.virginia.edu/harlem/JohMakiF.html.

Migration, as it became known, completely changed the face of Manhattan. In 6 years, the black population of Harlem doubled from 50,000 to more than 100,000. One-quarter of the black population was from New York City, while another quarter came from foreign countries. The other half came from the South and the Midwest. By 1930, Harlem's black population had exceeded 200,000.

"Father of Harlem"

Harlem's residents were almost entirely white in 1901, when two landlords who lived next to each other got into

Shown here in the center is Philip A. Payton Jr.'s home. Known as "the father of Harlem," he lived there from 1903 to his death in 1917.

an argument. What started the disagreement is a mystery, but it ended up changing history. One landlord decided to anger his rival by hiring Philip A. Payton Jr. to fill his empty building with black tenants. Payton, a porter who desperately wanted to become the city's first African American real estate agent, saw his chance. He had no problem finding tenants—there was an extreme housing shortage for black people in Manhattan because few landlords would rent to them. Payton managed the property and convinced other landlords to let him manage their houses and apartments.

In 1903, Payton was so successful that he spent $500,000 (equal to $13.3 million in 2018) to found the Afro-American Realty Company in downtown Manhattan. Within a few years, Payton was known as "the father of Harlem," having changed the racial character of the neighborhood almost single-handedly. Payton's company failed a few years later, but by that time, other black real estate agents were following in his footsteps. Not only were black people moving into apartments, they were also purchasing properties in the neighborhood.

Not everyone was happy with Harlem's black migration. White residents began fleeing in large numbers from what they called the "Negro Invasion." Many white residents felt that having black neighbors lowered their social status and property value.

The black community was then able to purchase or rent the vacated properties. By 1911, black Americans had purchased 10 percent of Harlem's large apartment buildings, called tenements, and 40 percent of its private homes. As black real estate agent John Royall stated, "the colored people are in Harlem to stay."[4]

Creating Legends

Even as real estate prices were falling, the economic picture was improving for many people living in Harlem. In 1914, World War I began in Europe. Even before the United States joined the fight and declared war on Germany in April 1917, the government was active in aiding its European allies. Wartime industries were ordered to produce a record number of armaments, clothes, rations, and other goods. At the same time, the war cut off the steady supply of white laborers who had been immigrating from Europe to New York since the 1880s. This created a labor shortage, and some employers began hiring black laborers. Even more black southerners began leaving the rural South.

For the first time, black laborers were making good wages, saving money, and investing in real estate. By 1920, it was not unusual for a black family to walk into a real estate office and put down anywhere from $1,000 to $5,000 in cash to purchase property.

Some of the stories of black entrepreneurs making fortunes in real estate are legendary. In 1925,

From neighborhood food businesses to city-wide real estate brokerages, the opportunities available to black Harlem residents stood in stark contrast to many parts of America at the time.

James Weldon Johnson wrote a story about Lillian Harris Dean, known as "Pig Foot Mary." She had become successful by selling "soul food," such as fried chicken and pickled pig's feet, from a small stand in Harlem. Johnson wrote,

"Pig Foot Mary" is a character in Harlem. Everybody who knows

the corner of Lenox Avenue and One Hundred and Thirty-fifth Street knows "Mary" and her stand and has been tempted by the smell of her pigsfeet, fried chicken and hot corn, even if he has not been a customer. "Mary" ... bought the five-story apartment house at the corner of Seventh Avenue and One Hundred and Thirty-seventh Street at a price of $42,000. Later she sold it to the Y.W.C.A. for dormitory purposes ... [for] $72,000.[5]

Dozens of success stories of this type abounded in the neighborhood. The total value of property owned by black Americans in Harlem in 1925 exceeded $60 million. The buying and selling created some of the first black real estate moguls in New York history. Johnson wrote,

[This is] amazing, especially when we take into account the short time in which [it happened]. Twenty years ago Negroes were begging for the privilege of renting a flat in Harlem. Fifteen years ago, barely a half dozen colored men owned real property in all Manhattan. And down to ten years ago, the amount that had

been acquired in Harlem was comparatively negligible. Today [1925] Negro Harlem is practically owned by Negroes.[6]

A Cultural Rebirth

With poverty rates falling and property ownership rising, the stage was set for a cultural rebirth in Harlem. All that was needed was a trigger to set it all in motion. Many believe that the catalyst of the New Negro movement was a victory parade held on February 17, 1919, several months after the end of World War I. On that sunny winter morning, approximately 1,300 veterans of the all-black 369th Infantry Regiment marched up Fifth Avenue alongside their military jazz band.

The infantry, named the "Hellfighters," was made up of the first black troops sent to fight on the European battlefront in World War I. They spent 191 continuous days engaged in trench warfare, and their valor was legendary on both sides of the conflict. While the German enemy called them the *"Blutlustige Schwarze Männer,"* or "bloodthirsty black men," the French called them heroes. The 369th was the only American unit awarded the Croix de Guerre, the French High Command's highest mark of honor. The marching Harlem Hellfighters were led by the regiment's 60-piece band under the direction of Lieutenant James Reese Europe. "Big Jim" Europe had been a legendary trumpeter before the war.

Just as the Hellfighters beat the German enemy, Big Jim's jazz compositions conquered audiences in France, Belgium, and England. On that spectacular February morning, hundreds of thousands of adoring Americans stood in the streets or waved flags from office windows as the Hellfighters marched with military precision up Fifth Avenue.

The white audiences downtown applauded politely for the black soldiers, but after they crossed over to Lenox and entered Harlem, they received a true heroes' welcome. Girlfriends and relatives joined the ranks of soldiers, and a torrent of pennants, flags, banners, and scarves rained down on the men. According to the newspaper *New York Age*,

Never in the history of [New York] has such a rousing royal welcome been given returning heroes from the field of battle; not for many a day is it likely that thousands of white and colored citizens will participate in such a tumultuous and enthusiastic demonstration ...

In Harlem the greeting bordered on riot ... Playing "Here Comes My Daddy Now," the [Hellfighters] marched between two howling walls of humanity ...

Those unable to secure standing room on the sidewalk [hung from windows and lampposts], while from the rooftops, thousands stood and whooped things up.[7]

The Harlem Hellfighters were among 380,000 black Americans who served during World War I. These soldiers faced severe discrimination and segregation within the military. After spending time in France, the black soldiers discovered they had more rights in Europe than they did in the United States. In the Chicago African American newspaper *Defender* in 1919, Lieutenant William N. Colson wrote,

While in France, the Negro soldiers ... discovered that the only white men that treated them as men were native Europeans, and especially the French with their wider social experience and finer social sense. The Frenchman was unable to comprehend American color prejudice. The Englishman was much more democratic than the American.[8]

This fair treatment helped the heroes of Harlem return home with a new sense of dignity. They were done cowering under white racism and were willing to take risks to prove their worth to a society that had never valued their contributions.

Beginning the Fight for Equal Rights

Black veterans were among the most eager to fight for equal rights after the war. However, there was a political divide within the black American community. On one side, older black leaders such as William Edward Burghardt (W. E. B.) Du Bois, cofounder of the National Association for the Advancement of Colored People (NAACP), worked with white supporters who believed that nonviolence was the path to equal rights and integration. Some felt Du Bois's efforts were geared toward helping the small number of middle-class black Americans and professionals. This alienated young black radicals who called themselves "New Negroes" to distinguish themselves from traditional leaders. The New Negroes did not necessarily believe in integration. Many believed violence was the only solution to their problems. This new posture was clearly defined by Oklahoma publisher Roscoe Dunjee, who wrote in the newspaper *Black Dispatch,*

> *The New Negro, who stands today released in spirit, finds himself, in America ... physically bound and shackled by LAWS AND CUSTOMS THAT WERE MADE FOR SLAVES, and all of the unrest ... charged to my people IS THE BATTLE OF FREE MEN POUNDING ON WALLS THAT SURROUND THEM.*[9]

The New Negroes supported black nationalism and black liberation, movements that struck fear in the hearts of the white establishment. Black nationalists believed African Americans should be proud of their heritage and advocated building separate communities based on black pride. Black war veterans, who were leading members of the New Negro movement, were ready to fight back against the KKK and other vigilantes who were lynching African Americans on a regular basis in the South. Colson summed up the feelings of many when he wrote, "The next war for democracy [will] be in the land of 'THE STAR SPANGLED BANNER.'"[10]

Marcus Garvey's Pan-Africanism

The indisputable leader of the New Negro movement was not a war veteran or a southerner but a Jamaican immigrant. Marcus Garvey moved to the United States in 1916. The following year, he established the headquarters of the Universal Negro Improvement Association (UNIA) in Harlem. The UNIA began with 13 members, including Garvey, but quickly grew beyond the borders of Harlem. Garvey preached a "Back to Africa" or Pan-African message, calling for all black people to move to Africa and start their own free nation. Garvey's philosophy is often called "Garveyism."

Any person of African descent could join UNIA for 35 cents and a pledge to support the association. Within months of its founding, the UNIA swelled to 12,000 members. By 1918, its influential newspaper had a circulation of 500,000. In 1920, Garvey claimed there were 3 million UNIA members in the United States, Central and South America, and the Caribbean. While some experts believe Garvey inflated the membership numbers, there is little doubt that the UNIA had a powerful influence in Harlem, where about one out of every three residents belonged to the organization.

Taking advantage of his widespread support, Garvey planned several money-making projects to pay for his dream of founding an independent black nation. He promoted black nationalism by providing employment and economic independence through several successful business ventures in Harlem. These businesses, which were staffed and run by black Americans, were financed through donations. Garvey's Negro Factories Corporation (NFC) established everything from laundries and restaurants to hotels, printers, and even a factory that specialized in making African American dolls.

Within months, the NFC became a symbol of African American business expertise in Harlem. The company's businesses competed successfully with white-owned businesses, and the stores provided employment for Harlem residents who were denied elsewhere. Hundreds of men and women found work as managers, clerks, accountants, stenographers, and secretaries. In addition, women were often put in positions of authority, which was considered quite unusual during an era when men dominated business and politics.

The NFC invested in real estate, offices, and empty factories and then rented them at a discount to faltering black-owned businesses. Garvey considered their success important to the black independence movement. In 1920 he wrote,

All these [financial achievements] to the ordinary optimist would seem a miracle, but all these things have been accomplished through the determination of the men and women who banded themselves together as members of the movement. Wherever there is a will there is a way, and the will of the New Negro is to do or die.[11]

Harlem Royalty

Nowhere was the New Negro movement more on display than the first UNIA convention, held in Harlem in August 1920. The event attracted 25,000 members. They named Garvey "His Excellency the Provisional President of Africa." In this role, he claimed to represent the African government in exile and act as leader of all black people throughout the world. Garvey created his own Harlem royalty, bestowing titles such as Duke of the Nile and Viscount of Niger on his closest advisers. Bearers of these titles—and Garvey himself—appeared in military-style uniforms bedecked with medals and decorations,

Marcus Garvey (shown here) was an inspiration for many African Americans. He inspired the creation of groups such as the Nation of Islam and the Rastafari movement.

all tailor-made by the NFC. The UNIA also adopted a national flag—a red, black, and green banner said to represent the motherland, Africa.

After the opening ceremonies, the UNIA convention hosted a three-hour parade through Harlem that was grander than the one that welcomed the return of the Hellfighters. The uniformed Harlem royalty led 50,000 UNIA members in a procession that stretched 10 city blocks. Garvey was the central focus, regally seated in a Packard convertible and wearing a purple, green, and black uniform festooned with gold braids and a hat with red plumes. Supporters carried signs reading, "Garvey the Negro Moses—Long May He Live" and "The Negro Fought in Europe, He Can Fight in Africa."[12]

Garvey's Critics

Not all black Americans thought Garvey was a positive leader. The pomp, ceremony, and public adulation frightened many traditional black leaders who disagreed with Garvey's combination of politics and self-promotion. Du Bois was especially critical, calling Garvey a "little fat black man, ugly … with … a big head,"[13] and noting that some had invested their entire life savings in Garvey's various stock market offerings. In a 1921 article in *Crisis*, the NAACP's newspaper, Du Bois wrote,

[Garvey is] a stubborn, domineering leader of the mass; he has worthy industrial and commercial schemes but he is an inexperienced businessman. His … methods are bombastic, wasteful, illogical and ineffective and almost illegal.[14]

Du Bois was not the only person examining the business practices of the UNIA. Garvey's Pan-African message frightened many within the U.S. government who feared a violent black uprising. The Federal Bureau of Investigation (FBI), the State Department, the U.S. Postal Service, and even military intelligence agents used the threat as an excuse to spy on Garvey. They broke into his offices and infiltrated the UNIA. Postmaster General Roger Bowen stated that Garvey planned "to instill into the minds of negroes … that they have been greatly wronged and oppressed by the white races and that they can only hope for relief and redress through concerted and aggressive action on their part."[15]

In 1922, Garvey was formally charged with using the U.S. Postal Service to defraud buyers of UNIA stock. He was convicted and imprisoned in a federal penitentiary in Atlanta, Georgia. In 1925, President Calvin Coolidge shortened his sentence, and Garvey was released in 1927 and deported to Jamaica, where many people still thought of him as a hero and freedom fighter.

Garvey spent much of the Harlem Renaissance fighting what some saw as prejudicial persecution by the U.S.

government. After Garvey went to jail, his wife, Amy Jacques Garvey, kept the UNIA alive, and the group's philosophies provided a strong political foundation for the Harlem Renaissance. By promoting racial consciousness and a powerful sense of independence and black pride, Garvey's philosophies provided hope in a time of despair. In part, Garvey's messages of pride helped inspire the writers, artists, and musicians who would become the faces of the Harlem Renaissance.

Chapter Two

THE WRITTEN WORDS OF THE RENAISSANCE

Elementary school teacher Sonje Sturdivant wanted her students to learn about the Harlem Renaissance, but she wanted it to be more than just an ordinary lesson. A teacher at Robertson Charter School in Illinois, Sturdivant decided to help her class raise money for a new display about the time period for Decatur, Illinois's African-American Cultural and Genealogical Society Museum. The students raised more than $1,000 for the exhibit. "We thought it was a great idea to teach the kids about this period of rebirth in the arts as well as the political and social areas," Sturdivant said. "There were a lot of people from that era this generation won't know about unless [we] expose them to these kids." For these kids, the Harlem Renaissance was not just a chapter in a history textbook. As one fourth-grader said, "It feels real to me now."[16] In addition to fund-raising, the class did research projects about the

Harlem Renaissance, dressed in period clothing, and read some of the poetry from that time.

While music, art, and theater were essential parts of the Harlem Renaissance, the intellectual basis for the entire movement came from the writers. These men and women were the leaders of Harlem's so-called Talented Tenth, the 10 percent of the neighborhood residents that were successful doctors, lawyers, publishers, musicians, actors, and authors.

The writers of what was called the Negro Literary Renaissance were aware that the world was watching—and reading—their works. This awareness led them to focus on achieving their goals of increasing interest in black history and culture and promoting racial pride.

The promoters of the Harlem Renaissance were inspired by a previous generation who had written about their African heritage and black American folk culture

A Double Self

*T*he *Souls of Black Folk*, written in 1903 by W. E. B. Du Bois, was extremely influential among the writers of the Harlem Renaissance. In the excerpt below, Du Bois examined the experience of being both black and American:

> *The history of the American Negro is the history of this strife,—this longing to attain self-conscious manhood, to merge his double self into a better and truer self. In this merging he wishes neither of the older selves to be lost. He would not Africanize America, for America has too much to teach the world and Africa. He would not bleach his Negro soul in a flood of white Americanism, for he knows that Negro blood has a message for the world. He simply wishes to make it possible for a man to be both a Negro and an American, without being cursed and spit upon by his fellows, without having the doors of Opportunity closed roughly in his face.[1]*

1. W. E. B. Du Bois, *The Souls of Black Folk*. Chicago, IL: McClurg, 1903. www.bartleby.com/114/1.html.

in the late 1890s. For example, the American Negro Academy (ANA), founded in Washington, D.C., in 1897, brought together black intellectuals who promoted African American literature, arts, music, and history.

As an outgrowth of the ANA's work, by the 1910s, there were at least 500 newspapers and magazines in the United States devoted to black social, historical, and cultural issues. In 1915, Carter Woodson, a Harvard PhD, cofounded the Association for the Study of Negro Life and History, the first black historical association. This organization publishes the *Journal of African American History* (originally named the *Journal of Negro History*) and originally promoted Negro History Week, which grew into Black History Month. This event is still recognized throughout the United States and Canada each February, and in October in the United Kingdom (UK).

Two Conflicting Worlds

W. E. B. Du Bois was among the scholars who wrote papers for the ANA in its early years, and his 1903 book, *The Souls of Black Folk*, was extremely influential. In the book, Du Bois put forth the idea that African Americans are torn between two conflicting worlds—their African heritage

W. E. B. Du Bois took on many roles, including educator, historian, writer, editor, poet, and civil rights activist. At the age of 95, he became a naturalized citizen of Ghana.

and their American homeland:

> [The] Negro is … born with a veil, and gifted with second-sight in this American world,—a world which yields him no true self-consciousness, but only lets him see himself through the revelation of the [American] world. It is a peculiar sensation, this double-consciousness, this sense of always looking at one's self through the eyes of others, of measuring one's soul by the tape of a world that looks on in amused contempt and pity. One ever feels his two-ness,—an American, a Negro; two souls, two thoughts, two unreconciled strivings; two warring ideals in one dark body, whose dogged strength alone keeps it from being torn asunder.[17]

Harlem Renaissance writers Langston Hughes and James Weldon Johnson both credited *The Souls of Black Folk* for inspiring them in their early years. Hughes said it was "my earliest memory of any book … except a schoolbook,"[18] while Johnson said it was "a work which … has had a greater effect upon and within the Negro race in America than any other single [book] published."[19]

Claude McKay

When poet Claude McKay read Du Bois's *The Souls of Black Folk* in 1912, he said, "it shook me like an earthquake."[20] Born in Jamaica, McKay too felt that he was torn between his African roots and the traditions of the white colonists who governed his homeland. Living in Harlem in 1919, McKay was among the first poets to encapsulate the experiences of the black urban masses. He wrote "If We Must Die" during a period known as the Red Summer of 1919, when 25 race riots occurred in major American cities including Charleston, South Carolina; Washington, D.C.; and Chicago. The riots were largely attacks on black neighborhoods by unemployed white Americans who were angry that black laborers had taken many factory jobs. During the Red Summer, 43 black men were lynched, 8 were burned at the stake, and hundreds died from other racial violence.

In this excerpt from "If We Must Die," McKay called for aggressive self-defense against the rioters:

> If we must die, let it not be like hogs
>
> Hunted and penned in an
>   inglorious spot,
>
> While round us bark the mad and
>   hungry dogs,
>
> Making their mock at our
>   accursed lot …
>
> O kinsmen we must meet the
>   common foe!
>
> Though far outnumbered let us show
>   us brave,
>
> And for their thousand blows deal
>   one deathblow!

Claude McKay's Harlem Shadows *was praised by literary critics and focused on racial questions and problems.*

*What though before us lies the
    open grave?*

*Like men we'll face the murderous,
    cowardly pack,*

*Pressed to the wall, dying, but
    fighting back!*[21]

McKay, who was 30 at the time the poem was published, expressed similar sentiments in his book *Harlem Shadows*, which included more than 60 poems, such as "America," "The White City," "In Bondage," "Enslaved," "Outcast," and "The Lynching."

His book of poetry made McKay the most celebrated black poet in the United States at the time. In the *New Republic* magazine, white critic Robert Littel discussed *Harlem Shadows* and also acknowledged the talents of James Weldon Johnson. Littel concluded that the two authors "make me sit up and take notice when they write about their race and ours. They strike hard and pierce deep. It is not merely poetic emotions they express, but something fierce and constant, icy cold, and white hot."[22]

In Story and Song

James Weldon Johnson was one of the most successful African American writers in the United States. Born in 1871, he had enrolled in the all-black Atlanta University at the age of 16, and in 1897, he was the first African American to take the Florida Bar Exam to become a lawyer. Segregation in the South weighed heavily on Johnson, so he began writing song lyrics with his brother Rosamond. The brothers traveled to New York in 1899 to sell their work, and within a few years, the Johnson brothers were a successful songwriting team. Songs such as "The Congo Love Song" and "Under the Bamboo Tree" were so popular that people bought hundreds of thousands of copies of the sheet music, making the Johnsons wealthy men. Their song "Lift Every Voice and Sing," about liberty bringing a new day after the dark night of slavery, became an instant classic. Written in 1900 to commemorate the anniversary of President Abraham Lincoln's birthday, the song became known as the "Negro National Hymn" and is still widely sung today.

In 1912, Johnson published the novel *The Autobiography of an Ex-Colored Man* about a light-skinned African American man who passed himself off as white, married a white woman, and had two children. The plot was extremely controversial for the time, and Johnson published it anonymously.

Like the conflicted subjects of *The Souls of Black Folk*, the protagonist in Johnson's book was filled with self-doubt about his African American identity. He rejected his identity after witnessing a vicious lynching, shamed that he belonged to a race that could be treated in such a manner. However, after reading books by Frederick Douglass and other black inspirational

An Ongoing Dilemma

Several black writers of the Harlem Renaissance became quite popular in the 1920s; however, their books were published by a white New York literary establishment for white audiences. Therefore, many African American authors had to consider the racial prejudices of their white readers to be successful. In his 1928 essay, "The Dilemma of the Negro Author," James Weldon Johnson explained the issue:

> If the Negro author selects white America as his audience, he is bound to run up against … a whole row of hard-set stereotypes which are not easily broken up. White America has some firm opinions as to what the Negro is, and consequently some pretty well fixed ideas as to what should be written about him, and how.
>
> What is the Negro in the artistic conception of white America? In the brighter light, he is a simple, indolent, docile, improvident peasant; a singing, dancing, laughing, weeping child; picturesque beside his log cabin and in the snowy fields of cotton; naïvely charming with his banjo and his songs in the moonlight and along the lazy Southern rivers; a faithful, ever-smiling and genuflecting old servitor to the white folks of quality; a pathetic and pitiable figure …
>
> Ninety-nine one-hundredths of all that has been written about the Negro in the United States in three centuries and read with any degree of interest or pleasure by white America has been written in conformity to one or more of these ideas.[1]

1. James Weldon Johnson, "The Dilemma of the Negro Author," in *The Harlem Renaissance 1920–1940, vol. 2, The Politics and Aesthetics of "New Negro" Literature,* Cary D. Wintz, ed. New York, NY: Garland, 1996, p. 248.

figures, the character comes to appreciate black culture with its musical and storytelling traditions. The plot takes an autobiographical turn when the character, like Johnson, becomes a composer and ragtime piano player, writing songs that blend American music with black spiritual traditions to present a positive image of African Americans to the world.

Production of Great Literature and Art

Although *The Autobiography of an Ex-Colored Man* only found a small audience when it was published, Johnson continued to write fiction, nonfiction, and poetry. As editor of the newspaper *New York Age*, he wrote the influential "Views and Reviews" column between 1915 and 1923. During this period, Johnson published *The Book of American Negro Poetry* with the words of 31 black poets, most of whom were unknown. In the preface to the book, Johnson stated that stereotypes of African American inferiority could be easily disproved if people were only aware of the contributions black people have made to the arts. He said,

> *The public, generally speaking, does not know that there are American Negro poets …*
>
> *It is a matter which has a direct bearing on the most vital of American problems.*
>
> *A people may become great through many means, but there is only one measure by which its greatness is recognized and acknowledged. The final measure of the greatness of all peoples is the amount and standard of the literature and art they have produced. The world does not know that a people is great until that people produces great literature and art. No people that has produced great literature and*

> *art has ever been looked upon by the world as distinctly inferior …*
>
> *And nothing will do more to … raise his status than a demonstration of intellectual parity by the Negro through the production of literature and art.*[23]

Johnson wrote about black contributions to music, including spirituals, ragtime, and dance crazes. He also wrote about the 19th-century black folktales and poetry. Johnson's overall theme, that black music, dance, and literature would undermine racism, was one of the guiding forces behind the Harlem Renaissance.

Dialect in Literature

Although he promoted black literature, Johnson believed that African American authors should avoid writing in black dialect, which was seen as the speech of the uneducated in inferior classes. This dialect came in two forms. The first was the stereotypical speech of poor southern black Americans who said "gwine" instead of "going," "ma" instead of "my," and "mo" for "more." The other black dialect, called Harlemese or "jive," was more controversial and judged like some rap music is today. Johnson called jive "the common, racy, living authentic speech of the Negro in … real life."[24] It was the language of jazz musicians or "hep cats," who called New York City "the Apple," with the main stem of the Apple being Harlem. To use one's brain

Langston Hughes was a famous poet during the Harlem Renaissance who was known for writing in dialect.

or apply oneself diligently to a task was called "busting your conk." Someone wearing fancy clothes was "togged to the bricks."

While some authors believed that using black dialects degraded African Americans, many of Harlem's writers thought otherwise. Langston Hughes, who has been called a jazz poet because of the rhythmic, moving character of his words, made a name for himself writing in dialect. Hughes's first major poem "The Weary Blues" won first prize in the poetry competition held by the literary magazine *Opportunity: A Journal of Negro Life* in 1925. This excerpt describes a man listening to an old blues musician in Harlem:

Droning a drowsy syncopated tune,

*Rocking back and forth to a
    mellow croon,*

I heard a Negro play.

*Down on Lenox Avenue the
    other night …*

*With his ebony hands on each
    ivory key*

*He made that poor piano moan
    with melody …*

*I heard that Negro sing, that old
    piano moan—*

"Ain't got nobody in all this world,

Ain't got nobody but ma self.

I's gwine to quit ma frownin'

And put ma troubles on the shelf."[25]

Reviewers loved "The Weary Blues" and Hughes's first book of poetry, but when he published his second book of poems, *Fine Clothes to the Jew*, it was highly criticized. The title, which upset Jewish people, refers to a man who was so poor he had to pawn his suit for a few nickels. The main criticism, however, came from the black press because of the way Hughes portrayed the reality of black urban life. As Hughes recalled in his 1940 autobiography, *The Big Sea*, black critics called the book

a disgrace to the race, a return to the dialect tradition, and a parading of all our racial defects before the public …

In anything white people were likely to read, [black intellectuals] wanted to put their best foot forward, their politely polished and cultural foot— and only that foot … [When] Negroes wrote books they wanted them to be books in which only good Negroes, clean and cultured and not-funny Negroes, beautiful and nice and upper class were presented.[26]

Reaction was fierce: "The Pittsburgh *Courier* ran a big headline across the top of the page, *LANGSTON HUGHES' BOOK OF POEMS TRASH*. The headline in the New York *Amsterdam News* was *LANGSTON HUGHES—THE SEWER DWELLER*." The Chicago *Whip* called Hughes "the poet low-rate of Harlem,"[27] which made a play on the words "poet laureate," a title of respect.

A Time of Soul-Searching

In his defense, Hughes argued that while he sympathized with the critics' point of view, he did not know anybody who was "wholly beautiful and wholly good."[28] Being of modest means himself, he did not know what life was like for upper-class black Americans, such as those who attended the elite universities and listened to classical music, so he wrote about his life and the people who populated it.

Hughes was gaining fame during a period that was particularly sensitive for black authors. For the first time, the powerful New York publishing world was paying close attention, and there was much soul-searching among authors as to how they portrayed African Americans.

In 1923, a mainstream, national publishing company printed Jean Toomer's *Cane*, an experimental novel mixing poetry and narrative prose about African American life in the rural South and urban North. *Cane* not only describes injustice and prejudice with angry prose, but also describes the beauty of black culture. Commenting on the quality of Toomer's writing, critic William Stanley Braithwaite wrote, "*Cane* is a book of gold and bronze, of dusk and flame, of ecstasy and pain, and Jean Toomer is a bright morning star of a new day of the Race in literature."[29]

In 1924, another major publishing house released Jessie Fauset's book, *There Is Confusion*, which depicts the lives of middle-class African American families from a woman's perspective. Fauset's characters are based on the world she knew. They had been in the United States for many generations, were somewhat affluent, and, like many white families of that era, placed great importance on class, pedigree, and manners. Fauset based her novel on her belief that middle-class black and white Americans shared more cultural similarities than was widely acknowledged. In regards to her 1931 work *The Chinaberry Tree: A Novel of American Life*, she said, "I have depicted something of the home life of the colored American who is not being pressed too hard by the Furies of Prejudices, Ignorance, and Economic Injustice. And behold he is not so vastly different from any other American."[30]

As publishers were considering *The Chinaberry Tree*, it received much of the same objection as *There Is Confusion* did. One publisher who had rejected *There Is Confusion* scoffed, "White readers just don't expect Negroes to be like this."[31]

The Formal Launch of the Negro Literary Renaissance

Writer and sociologist Charles S. Johnson hoped to address the perception gap between black and white by planning a banquet to celebrate the publication of Fauset's novel. Johnson was editor of

Opportunity: A Journal of Negro Life, the official publication of the National Urban League (NUL), an organization founded to help advance the economic interests of black Americans.

On March 21, 1924, Johnson hosted the NUL Civic Club Dinner. Harlem stars Langston Hughes, poet Countee Cullen, and James Weldon Johnson were honored along with Fauset. Johnson also invited white writers, editors, and critics from New York's powerful literary establishment. This event, attended by more than 100 people, stimulated great interest in black writers among white publishers and is considered the formal launching of the Negro Literary Renaissance. Looking back on the event in later years, Hughes was prompted to write, "Charles Johnson did more to encourage and develop Negro writers during the 1920s than anyone else in America."[32]

Paul U. Kellogg, one of the attendees at the Civic Club Dinner, was editor of the *Survey Graphic,* a popular illustrated magazine that focused on poverty, racism, education, working conditions, political reform, and other sociological issues. Inspired by the burgeoning black literary movement, Kellogg decided to devote the entire March 1925 issue of the magazine to the art and literature of Harlem. The "Harlem Issue" was edited by writer, philosopher, and educator Alain Locke and remains one of the most detailed accounts of that era. The issue was so successful that Locke expanded it into a book, *The New Negro,* which explored the Harlem Renaissance's writing, art, and literary criticism. In the introduction to the book, Locke explained the significance of the movement:

> *Negro life is not only establishing new contacts and founding new centers, it is finding a new soul. There is a fresh spiritual and cultural focusing. We have, as a heralding sign, an unusual outburst of creative expression. There is a renewed race-spirit that consciously and proudly sets itself apart. Justifiably then, we speak of the offerings of this book embodying these ripening forces as culled from the first fruits of the Negro Renaissance.*[33]

"Fy-ah Gonna Burn Ma Soul!"

Along with authors Cullen, McKay, Toomer, and Hughes, a number of important writers were part of the Harlem Renaissance. One of the most vivacious, or energetic, members of the group, Zora Neale Hurston, was a latecomer to the renaissance. Historians state Hurston was born in 1891 in Notasulga, Alabama, but she claimed to be 10 years younger and born in Eatonville, Florida. At the time, Hurston was known more for her humor, use of old-style slave dialect, and outsized charm than her literary accomplishments. Most of her critically acclaimed work was written in the 1930s after the formal end of the Harlem Renaissance.

Hurston contributed several short stories to magazines while attending Barnard College, and people began to

When people think of the Harlem Renaissance, Zora Neale Hurston's work often comes to mind.

take notice of her work. After moving to Harlem in 1925, the independent, outspoken woman with a rich, commanding voice quickly became a central figure in the Harlem literary scene.

Stories of Hurston's exploits are legendary. She smoked cigarettes in public, which was considered disgraceful for a woman at the time. On one occasion, she took a nickel from the cup of a blind beggar for bus fare, promising to repay it later. She also lived in a house full of men, including other writers and artists, which many considered scandalous at the time. Theophilius Lewis wrote about the parties at this house in his newspaper column:

> The story goes out that the bathtubs in the house [are] always packed with sourmash [whiskey], while gin [flows] from all the water taps and the flush boxes [behind the toilets are] filled with ... beer ... a great deal more smoke [comes] out of the windows than [is] warranted by the size of the fire in the [furnace].[34]

The allusion to smoke might have inspired Hurston, Wallace Thurman, Richard Nugent, and painter Aaron Douglas to collaborate on the magazine *Fire!!* in 1926. Although short-lived, the magazine was the only publication of its kind during the Harlem Renaissance, produced by the movement's artists and writers.

According to Hughes, the group chose the title *Fire!!* because they wanted to "burn up a lot of the old, dead conventional Negro-white ideas of the past."[35] It featured articles mocking and scorning the literary establishment, celebrating jazz and blues music, and discussing forbidden topics such as homosexuality and pagan (a system outside of the main world religions) beliefs. The foreword to the magazine was enough to frighten some readers. It said,

> FIRE ... flaming, burning, searing, and penetrating far beneath
>
> the superficial items of the flesh to boil

> the sluggish blood.
>
> FIRE ... a cry of conquest in the night, warning those who sleep
>
> and revitalizing those who linger in the quiet places dozing.
>
> FIRE ... melting steel and iron bars, poking livid tongues between
>
> stone apertures and burning wooden opposition with a crackling
>
> chuckle of contempt.
>
> FIRE ... weaving vivid, hot designs upon an ebon bordered loom
>
> and satisfying pagan thirst for beauty unadorned ... the flesh is
>
> sweet and real ... the soul an inward flush of fire ... Beauty? ...
>
> Flesh on fire—on fire in the furnace of life blazing ...
>
> Fy-ah,
>
> Fy-ah, Lawd,
>
> Fy-ah gonna burn ma soul![36]

Older black intellectuals, such as Du Bois, were shocked by the unseemly tone of the magazine. The literary critic for the *Baltimore Afro-American* sneered, "I have just tossed the first issue of *Fire* into

Painter Aaron Douglas was a contributor to the first and only issue of Fire!! *published during the Harlem Renaissance.*

the fire."[37]

The first and only issue cost the equivalent of $4,000 to produce, and it was nearly impossible to get white magazine dealers to distribute it. Ironically, the magazine came to an end when the copies were destroyed by a fire that swept through the apartment where they were stored. Many of the black writers who had contributed to *Fire!!* went on to have respectable careers as authors, poets, and educators. Hardened in the fires of prejudice, segregation, and disappointment, they provided a unique perspective on black life in the United States for generations to come. The impact and influence of *Fire!!* is clearly evidenced in the fact that, in January 2017, the magazine was revived and reissued. Titled *Fiyah*, it is subtitled "the magazine of black speculative fiction." The magazine's website lists the its mission:

What does it mean to be black and look at the intersectional issues of equality through the lens of science fiction and fantasy? ...

FIYAH rises from the ashes of the Black literary tradition started by Fire!! in 1926. We aren't here for respectability. We're here to ask what it means to be Black and extraordinary. We are a place to showcase your stories and grow your career ... we know you have stories to tell and we are here for it.[38]

Chapter Three

STRIDIN' AND STOMPIN'

When a piano player plays ragtime, their left hand works the bass notes and low chords of the piano, while their right hand quickly works the melody with rolling notes. This technique is known as "the Harlem Stride." While it was first used a century ago by musicians of the Harlem Renaissance, it is still a popular style for modern pianists, even though it represented the time period's "low art."

The Harlem Renaissance was split into two separate movements, known as the high and the low. Many works of art and literature during this period were created, in part, to prove to white society that African Americans were capable of making "high art," or art designed to appeal to intellectuals and contribute positively to American culture. As Charles S. Johnson, one of the leaders of the Harlem literary scene

said, African Americans could use the arts to make "a crack in the wall of racism."[39]

Conversely, "low art" revolved around loud, raucous jazz and blues played in speakeasies (hidden, illegal establishments that sold liquor during the Prohibition era), dance halls, and after-hours clubs. Many believed that low art was fueled by bootleg liquor, marijuana, and cocaine because the music was wild.

Black music had a much more significant cultural impact than literature had, causing a rift between some writers and musicians. Authors and poets, who were often called literati, of the time often considered jazz and blues music to be a low art, enforcing negative African American stereotypes. Musicians were amused by this opinion and even included the snobbish literati in their song lyrics.

The music called "low art" by some was incredibly popular with black and white audiences.

Some critics felt the music was a modern version of the racist minstrel shows from the 19th century. In these shows, black or white entertainers performed in blackface, which was theatrical makeup or burnt cork to give the appearance of dark skin. Black performers even had to wear blackface makeup on the stage because white audiences would not watch them without it. These minstrel shows mocked African Americans, stating they were lazy, superstitious, and only good for playing music or dancing.

The Power of Prohibition

Despite the literati, the Harlem Renaissance became known as part of the Jazz Age. The word "jazz" was originally a black slang term, but it became part of the American lexicon during the Roaring Twenties. Fashionable clothes were called "jazz dresses," and modern syncopated (a shifting of the normally accented rhythm in which the beat that is unaccented is stressed) verse was called "jazz poetry." However, first and foremost, jazz identified the swinging music that was heard everywhere in Harlem. It floated out of radios and record players in barbershops and beauty parlors. It was performed by live bands at dance halls, cabarets, and clubs. Soon, Harlem's sound was attracting white visitors to the area, including celebrities.

It was not just the music that brought white visitors to Harlem. In January 1919, the 18th Amendment was added to the U.S. Constitution, prohibiting the manufacture, sale, or transportation of alcoholic beverages. The law, known as Prohibition, profoundly influenced American life. It was illegal to purchase drinks such as a beer or a shot of whiskey, but millions of Americans broke this law. Many began making their own alcohol at home. Industrial grain alcohol and juniper were put into bottles and then topped with water from the tub, resulting in bathtub gin.

Those who did not make their own alcohol had to do business with criminals who imported, or bootlegged, alcohol from Canada and elsewhere. It was sold in illicit clubs called speakeasies, many of which were run by organized crime syndicates.

With the price of an illicit drink soaring from 25 cents in 1920 to $2 in 1925, hundreds of illegal drinking establishments opened on almost every block of Harlem. The illegal alcohol attracted adventurous young white people who spent money freely and danced to black jazz musicians playing the new dances, such as the black bottom and the Charleston.

Law enforcement officers, such as those shown here, confiscated alcohol during Prohibition.

Culture Clash

With a steady flow of wealthy customers, Harlem was booming with speakeasies, cellars, lounges, cafes, taverns, and supper clubs. With more than 125 entertainment places serving both black and white clientele, the African American character of Harlem quickly changed. The white visitors to Harlem did not represent the average

The citywide celebration of the 100th anniversary of the Harlem Renaissance in Columbus, Ohio, started as a simple idea from Nannette Maciejunes, the executive director of an art museum in Columbus.

In September 2015, Maciejunes attended a presentation by Wil Haygood, author of a 2016 biography of African American Supreme Court Justice Thurgood Marshall. She was inspired to ask Haygood if he would be willing to set up a Harlem Renaissance exhibit at her museum to celebrate its centennial. A few phone calls and three days later, the exhibit was being planned, and community organizations throughout Columbus wanted to be a part of it. The community-wide event, titled "I, Too, Sing America: The Harlem Renaissance at 100," began in January 2018 and was planned to run through January 2019. As Tom Katzenmeyer, president and CEO of the Greater Columbus Arts Council stated, "This is a massive collaboration and probably the most significant arts event in a long time."[1]

1. Ken Gordon, "Area Arts Groups to Mark 100th Anniversary of Harlem Renaissance in a Big Way," *The Columbus Dispatch*, December 4, 2017. www.dispatch.com/entertainmentlife/20171204/area-arts-groups-to-mark-100th-anniversary-of-harlem-renaissance-in-big-way.

American. Some said these customers were afflicted by "Harlemania," a nearly hysterical love of the area. Among those visiting Harlem in their expensive Stutz, Packard, or Daimler touring cars were Gertrude Vanderbilt Whitney (great-granddaughter of railroad magnate Cornelius Vanderbilt and founder of the Whitney Museum of American Art); French princess Violette Murat; German-born financier Otto Kahn; movie star Harold Lloyd; and Lady Patricia Mountbatten, the wife of British naval commander Lord Mountbatten. These people not only visited the "high" art establishments but also went "slumming" by going to "low-down" speakeasies.

One of the complications of this attention from high society was that black Americans were barred from several of the best restaurants, where only the staff and entertainers were black. A typical example was the gangster-owned Cotton Club, the country's most famous nightclub at the time. Located on Harlem's Lenox Avenue, the Cotton Club denied black people entry unless they were entertaining all-white crowds.

Many African Americans resented the white presence in their

The Cotton Club was owned by one of New York City's mob bosses, Owney Madden.

Hitting the Keys

Many residents of Harlem were unable to afford the expensive clubs patronized by white clientele and the Talented Tenth. Some were unable to afford rent and threw "rent parties," where attendees would crowd into an apartment and contribute 10 to 50 cents toward the host's rent. The parties lasted until dawn, and the entertainment could be spectacular. One of Harlem's leading piano players, or ticklers, Willie "the Lion" Smith described playing at one of these rent parties:

> Piano players called these affairs jumps or shouts ... It got so we never stopped and we were up and down Fifth, Seventh, and Lenox all night long hitting the keys ... On a single Saturday [we would] book as many as three parties ...
>
> There were, of course, some of the chitterling struts [parties] where a bunch of pianists would be in competition. [Our booking agent] Lippy was a great promoter and was always trying to steam up the guests to argue who was the best ... you had to stay by the keyboard to hold your own reputation for being a fast pianist ... During [the] early hours close to dawn the ... lights would be dimmed down and the people would call out to the piano player. "Play it, oh, play it," or "Break it down," or "Get in the gully and give us the everlovin' stomp." Those were happy days.[1]

1. Quoted in Jervis Anderson, *This Was Harlem*. New York, NY: Farrar Straus and Giroux, 1982, pp. 155–156.

neighborhood and the exclusionary policies, known as Jim Crow laws. According to Langston Hughes,

> Harlem Negroes did not like the Cotton Club and never appreciated its Jim Crow policy in the very heart of their dark community. Nor did ordinary Negroes like the growing influx of whites toward Harlem after sundown, flooding the little cabarets and bars where formerly only colored people laughed and sang, and where now the strangers were given the best ringside tables to sit and stare at the Negro customers—like amusing animals in a zoo.[40]

However, as Hughes also pointed

out, many of the clubs that banned African Americans were not successful. He said, "They failed to realize that a large part of the Harlem attraction for downtown New Yorkers lay in simply watching the colored customers amuse themselves."[41]

Tickling the Keys

The Harlem Renaissance offered steady employment to many talented black musicians and singers. There were at least 15 major jazz bands and 100 lesser-known ensembles that played in the neighborhood throughout the Roaring Twenties. These musicians were from all over the United States, and they helped create the true Harlem jazz sound.

The roots of jazz can be traced to late-19th-century New Orleans, where African American musicians blended several forms of traditional music, including work songs, blues, ragtime, Mardi Gras marches, and European military music to create a completely new sound. Ragtime was particularly favored in Harlem. In this style, pianists play complicated songs with the right hand, "tickling" the keys with the melody, while the left hand plays a complex section on the bass end.

Scott Joplin was considered the king of ragtime. His 1899 composition "Maple Leaf Rag" is believed to be the first instrumental music piece to sell more than 1 million copies of sheet music. Joplin moved to Harlem in 1907, and his music evolved into the "stride piano" style. The sound was so large and powerful that it could be compared to listening to a full orchestra. Joplin died in 1917, before the official start of the Harlem Renaissance.

The keyboardists called themselves "ticklers" but gave each other rowdy nicknames, such as "Bear," "Beetle," "Beast," and "Brute," based on their prowess on the piano. Harlem's most famous ticklers were Willie "the Lion" Smith, Ferdinand "Jelly Roll" Morton, and Fats Waller. However, New Jersey-born pianist James P. Johnson perfected the style in Harlem and earned the title "father of stride piano." As jazz musician and historian Mark C. Gridley explained in *Jazz Styles: History and Analysis*, Johnson "perfected the orchestral approach to jazz piano playing, as though he were a one-man band."[42] In addition to being a pianist, Johnson was a composer who wrote 230 songs, 19 symphonic works, and 11 musicals. His most famous composition was "The Charleston," which had an accompanying dance. This song brought jazz to a wider audience and became synonymous with the Jazz Age.

Sophisticated Music

Johnson often participated in contests with other notable stride players. These events, in which pianists attempted to cut each other down, or outplay each other with nearly impossible riffs and runs, attracted many young musicians.

Scott Joplin wrote dozens of songs between 1896 and 1917. Shown here is the cover for the sheet music for "Maple Leaf Rag," one of his most famous pieces.

Among them was up-and-coming pianist Edward "Duke" Ellington, who was awed by Johnson's creative licks, fast hands, and precision runs.

Ellington was born in Washington, D.C., in 1899 and moved to Harlem in 1923. Within a few years, he formed a red-hot band called the Washingtonians. Trumpet player Bubber Miley gave the Washingtonians a unique voice, wringing a down-and-dirty, blues-drenched, "gut bucket" sound from his horn. Ellington called it the "Jungle Sound," and it came to represent Harlem jazz.

By 1927, Ellington was pioneering a new type of jazz, composing music that mixed jazz with the lush orchestral sounds heard in popular theatrical musicals. By adding strings, brass, and woodwinds, Ellington forged a distinctive sound. Because Ellington's grand sound appealed to an upper-class white audience, critics called it "sophisticated music."

Ellington's new sound developed around the time his group was hired as the house band for the Cotton Club. The fashionable club was decorated in the style of a 19th-century southern mansion. Although it catered only to white people, all the entertainers and most of the staff were black. In addition, the employees were offensively portrayed as residents on a plantation or as savages. The owner's goal for the club's music and theme was to bring to mind the atmosphere of the jungle. However, these exclusionary and highly offensive policies reinforced stereotypes about African Americans.

The 14-piece band, now renamed Duke Ellington and His Cotton Club Orchestra, quickly achieved national recognition when it was featured on CBS radio broadcasts live from the club every Saturday night. With his newfound fame and money, Ellington was able to hire the best musicians in New York and write stunning arrangements that allowed them to showcase their talents.

Ellington played at the Cotton Club off and on until 1933. Between 1927 and 1931, his orchestra made 150 records. When not playing and recording in New York, Ellington toured extensively in the United States and Europe. Wherever he played, his manager, Irving Mills, sent out press releases that read: "Come on! Get hot! Get happy! [With] Harlem's jazz king, blaring, crooning, burning up the stage with his red hot rhythms, moaning saxophones, wailing cornets, laughing trombones, screaming clarinets."[43]

Ellington's many memorable compositions, including "Mood Indigo," "It Don't Mean a Thing If It Ain't Got That Swing," and "Sophisticated Lady," utilized catchy and unusual melodies. Although his strutting, swinging sounds became jazz classics across the globe, Ellington's music was firmly rooted in Harlem. In the late music professor Mark Tucker's essay, "Black Music in the Harlem Renaissance," he wrote,

Ellington's performances were broadcast on the radio each week, exposing his talents to a nationwide audience.

Even when touring took him away from home ... Ellington continued to celebrate Harlem in music. His compositions described its echoes and air shafts, boys and blue belles [beautiful women]. His songs advised people to drop off there and to slap their soles on Seventh Avenue. His signature piece ("Take the A Train") even told them which train to take [to reach Harlem]. And he paid tribute to his adopted community in "Beige" ... and in "A Tone Parallel to Harlem" ... a joyous evocation of Harlem's sounds, street-life, and citizens.[44]

A Different Kind of District

While Ellington's music crossed racial and cultural lines, the price of a night at the Cotton Club was daunting, often equal to a week's wages for the average New York resident. On the other hand, those who were not rich or white could find a wealth of entertainment in the "Jungle Alley" district. In *Harlem Speaks*, Cary D. Wintz described the district:

[Jungle Alley] provided a variety of entertainment options and a more eclectic and risqué environment. It catered to a racially mixed and ... uninhibited clientele. In Jungle Alley everyone rubbed shoulders—gay and straight, whites from across the city, working-class blacks as well as intellectuals, writers,

musicians, artists, businessmen, criminals, and prostitutes. They drank bootleg liquor, had access to marijuana and harder drugs, and danced or just listened to jazz and blues artists, often until daybreak.[45]

The "torrid warbler" Gladys Bentley was a typical entertainer in the district. Working at the Clam House, the vocalist sang suggestive songs while wearing a man's top hat and tuxedo. She sat at her piano from 10 p.m. until dawn, playing blues classics without stopping. According to Hughes, she played

with a powerful and continuous underbeat of jungle rhythm. Miss Bentley was an amazing exhibition of musical energy—a large, dark, masculine lady, whose feet pounded the floor while her fingers pounded the keyboard—a perfect piece of African sculpture, animated by her own rhythm.[46]

Bessie Smith: The Empress of the Blues

Bentley eventually became so popular she moved to bigger Harlem clubs, and then to Hollywood. She was only one of the Harlem blues singers to achieve international fame. Bessie Smith, known as "the Empress of the Blues," was among the biggest stars of the Harlem Renaissance.

Smith was born into dire poverty around 1892 in Chattanooga,

Tennessee. She was orphaned by age nine and earned a meager living dancing and singing on street corners accompanied by her brother on guitar. As a teenager, Smith was hired as a professional dancer in a black touring show whose star was the legendary singer Gertrude "Ma" Rainey, nicknamed "Mother of the Blues."

During an era when many black women were treated with even less respect than black men, Rainey carried herself as a proud diva. She sang about her life—bad times, relationship problems, and crippling loneliness—but demanded respect from her audiences. Smith gained the admiration of Rainey, and the two became inseparable, performing and writing songs together. By the early 1920s, both were major stars, playing together in theaters packed with integrated audiences.

In the early 1920s, most record companies refused to record black artists. However, after blues singer Mamie Smith (no relation to Bessie) had a few unexpected hits, record companies realized there was a huge demand for what they called "race records." Bessie Smith recorded "Down Hearted Blues" in 1923, and the record sold an astounding 780,000 copies that year. The money saved Columbia Records, which was nearly bankrupt, but Smith was only paid $250. In contrast, popular white artists such as Al Jolson were paid a royalty for each record sold and quickly became millionaires. Although her subsequent records sold

Bessie Smith continues to influence many modern singers who admire—and imitate—her passionate and funny songs.

millions, Smith primarily made her fortune as a performer, earning up to $2,000 a week playing various theaters in cities such as New York and Chicago. Describing her talents in their book *Black Magic*, Langston Hughes and Milton Meltzer wrote, "Bessie did not attempt to entertain. She simply stood still and shouted the blues without trick arrangements or orchestral refinements—and she rocked the joint. Before the days of microphones, Bessie could be heard for a mile."[47]

Smith was respected by many in Harlem. However, due to her lifestyle, she was shunned by the Harlem literati, who equated culture with European classical music and opera. According to jazz critic Chip Deffa, upper-class black Americans considered Smith "too much of the streets, a rough-edged reminder of lower-class roots they wanted to forget … Smith was a crude, primitive 'blues shouter' to be ignored."[48] Smith recognized these attitudes and responded in the 1933 song "Gimme a Pigfoot (and a Bottle of Beer)." In the lyrics, Smith scolded the highbrows for being tightly wound and for dismissing the blues. Instead, she called for a hot-stomping piano player and a party until dawn with soul food, beer, gin, and marijuana.

By this time, Smith's career was beginning to suffer. Many of her biggest fans were poor and could not afford to buy her records, thanks to the Great Depression, which began in 1929 and caused economic struggles for many people. When Smith recorded with jazz greats Jack Teagarden, Benny Goodman, and Leon Brown "Chu" Berry, however, she began moving beyond the blues and taking jazz in a new direction.

At the Savoy

With her low-down blues, Smith had difficulty competing with the lively jazz music that attracted massive crowds to the Savoy, Harlem's hottest nightspot. Covering an entire city block on Lenox Avenue, the Savoy opened in March 1926. Built by a white music promoter and a black businessman, the Savoy was an architectural wonder, featuring a huge lobby and a block-long dance hall atop two dazzling, mirror-lined marble staircases.

The dance palace was described as a community ballroom where black or white, rich or poor, local or tourist, could gain admission for only 50 cents on most nights and 75 cents on Sundays. In addition to drawing Harlem's blue-collar crowd of busboys, truck drivers, and domestic workers, the Savoy attracted royalty and movie stars, including the Prince of Wales, Marlene Dietrich, Greta Garbo, and Lana Turner. On weekends, up to 4,000 guests packed into the club to hear bands "stompin' at the Savoy."[49]

Fletcher Henderson and his Rainbow Orchestra was one of the world-class acts who played at the Savoy. Another star was drummer Chick Webb, leader of the Chick Webb Orchestra. Webb's

The Hottest Nightspot

The Savoy Ballroom was known as the Home of Happy Feet during the Harlem Renaissance. In their book *Black Magic*, Langston Hughes and Milton Meltzer explained,

> *In the Twenties it seemed as if all Harlem was dancing—and Harlemites set the rest of the world to dancing, too. The leg-flinging Charleston … originated with the kids of Harlem [and] swept the world … In quick succession for a decade new Negro dances followed, and some caught on with a wide public— the droll Black Bottom, the shim-sham-shimmy with its freeze-in-place break, the pixie-like truckin' raising a pointed finger, and above all the long popular Lindy hop originating at the Savoy Ballroom in 1927 … The Savoy in Harlem, an institution for many years, was a dance emporium known as the Home of Happy Feet, where downtown whites and uptown Negroes came to "trip the light fantastic," clap hands to the Charleston, to truck around the floor with arms akimbo, and to swing out in the Lindy hop, the dance that started the ballroom custom of couples not remaining close together as they as they dance. It was the Lindy that later turned into the rocking rhythms of the jitterbug.*[1]

1. Langston Hughes and Milton Meltzer, *Black Magic*. Englewood Cliffs, NJ: Prentice Hall, 1967, pp. 91–92.

driving beat was compared to a railroad train running at full throttle. The Savoy sponsored the "Battle of the Bands," where guest bands from New York, Chicago, and New Orleans were pitted against Webb's band. Even jazz greats such as Louis Armstrong, Cab Calloway, King Oliver, and Fess Williams feared battling Webb, who was often judged the winner by the cheering crowd.

Some of the best entertainment at the Savoy came from the dancers who strutted and jumped on the famous 50 by 250 feet (15 by 76 m) burnished maple and mahogany dance floor. The floor was used so much that it had to be replaced every three years. Many of the dance fads that swept across the country in the 1920s, such as the Lindy Hop, the Suzy Q, and the shim-sham shimmy, were invented at the Savoy, the "Home of Happy Feet."

On Tuesday nights, the club hosted the Savoy 400, featuring professional dancers such as George "Shorty"

The Savoy opened in March 1926 and closed in July 1958. It was an influential nightspot in Harlem that attracted many people and was the birthplace of many dances.

Snowden, who is often credited with naming the Lindy Hop. The Lindy Hop included pinwheel spins and "breakaways" in which the female dance partner was thrown and twirled high in the air with wild abandon. Swing dancers still perform the Lindy Hop today.

On Thursday nights, women were admitted free to the Savoy for "Kitchen Mechanics' Night," a slang term applied to cooks and maids. Saturday night was known as "Square Night" and was designed for the fumble-footed "unhip" white downtowners who showed up to crowd the dance floor.

The musicians of the Harlem Renaissance achieved two historically important goals. First, they introduced entirely new styles of playing and types of music to the world. Second, they gave black Americans and white Americans the chance to get to know each other in an entertaining and relaxed venue. This helped bridge— and then tear down—historic social and racial barriers. Supporting African American culture, including art, literature, theater, and music, became fashionable. Driven by the percussion and power of jazz music, the Harlem Renaissance reached a wider audience and made a permanent mark on the Roaring Twenties.

Chapter Four

THE RENAISSANCE ON THE STAGE

Langston Hughes wrote that the Harlem Renaissance officially began on May 23, 1921, when the musical revue *Shuffle Along* opened at the 63rd Street Music Hall above Times Square near Broadway. White people attended the show in droves, forcing police to convert 63rd Street into a one-way street to cope with the increased traffic.

Hughes called *Shuffle Along* "a honey of a show. Swift, bright, funny, rollicking, and gay, with a dozen danceable, singable tunes."[50] The revue was filled with comedy, ragtime music, and jazz dancing and ran for an astounding number of performances—what has been recorded as both 484 and 504, according to the Broadway *Playbill* website. It was the first major production in years to be produced, written, and performed entirely by African Americans.

Exploring Issues Through Theater

Eleven years before *Shuffle Along* premiered, black producers, directors, and actors were forming theater companies in Harlem. As early as 1910, black playwrights wrote dramas, comedies, and musicals for upper-class black audiences. These African American theater patrons could afford the tickets to Broadway shows but were either not allowed into the theaters or had to sit in the segregated balcony seats.

With black actors, dancers, and singers also largely banned on Broadway, Harlem productions attracted the most talented black performers in the United States. Many performed plays reflecting on their personal pain and beauty. As David Krasner wrote in his book *A Beautiful Pageant*, "Black theatre explored community issues away from white audiences and the demand to please them."[51]

In 2016, Shuffle Along *was briefly revived, starring Broadway legends Audra McDonald and Brian Stokes Mitchell (third and fourth from left, respectively).*

By 1914, there were several theaters in Harlem with their own repertory stock companies, or permanent groups of actors, directors, and stage technicians. The most famous, the Anita Bush Stock Company (later called the Lafayette Players), was founded by Lester Walton, amusement critic for *New York Age*, and Anita Bush, known as "the Little Mother of Negro Drama." The Lafayette Players presented a variety of entertainment, including musicals, comedies, grand operas, and William Shakespeare's plays. Their most popular productions, however, were uptown Harlem performances of downtown Broadway hits. These plays with all-black casts included classics such as *Dr. Jekyll and Mr. Hyde* and *The Count of Monte Cristo*. However, the play *Within the Law* was the one that attracted widespread attention when lawyer-turned-actor Clarence Muse mocked the common practice of white actors appearing in blackface makeup. Hughes and Meltzer explained,

The Lafayette Players were so popular that cofounder Anita Bush ended up founding similar theater groups in Chicago, Philadelphia, and the South.

Ebony dark Clarence Muse a great hit—performing the role of the lawyer in whiteface. Muse, who had enormous popularity with Harlem audiences and whose rich deep voice was well known, used a gimmick in [Within the Law] which never failed to bring the house down. At his

initial entrance, Muse first began to speak off stage, carrying on a brief conversation while still out of sight. The audience would think, "There comes Clarence," but they were unprepared for what was to happen—the very dark Muse stepped on stage completely white. Astonished pandemonium always broke out. Applause shook the theatre. Within the Law *in Harlem became an S.R.O. [standing room only] hit.*[52]

Muse later became a writer, director, and producer as well as one of the most famous black actors in Hollywood during the 1940s. However, Muse was just one among many fine actors in the company that included Abbie Mitchell, Laura Bowman, Charles Gilpin, Hilda Simms, and Frank Wilson. These actors were so talented that they began attracting white crowds from downtown. As Walton wrote in 1920,

It is beginning to dawn on the managers and actor folk on Broadway that something worthy of more than passing consideration to those interested in the drama is taking place weekly at the Lafayette Theatre further uptown. No longer are the Lafayette Players ... referred to in a jocular manner ... Nowadays stage celebrities in goodly numbers are wending their way to Seventh Avenue and 131st St. by limousine to look upon the efforts of these colored thespians with serious eye.[53]

Honing Their Skills

The Lafayette Players honed their skills in Harlem, but in April 1917, many of them participated in another groundbreaking event when they appeared in *Three Plays for the Negro Theatre* at the Garden Theater on Broadway. The three one act plays, written by white playwright Ridgely Torrence and produced with two white collaborators, featured an all-black cast of actors. James Weldon Johnson recalled the significance of this event in his 1930 book, *Black Manhattan*, writing that the opening of this performance was "the most important single event in the entire history of the Negro in the American theatre ... It was the first time anywhere in the United States the Negro actors in the dramatic theatre [commanded] the serious attention of the critics and of the general press and public."[54]

Three Plays for the Negro Theatre

did not run for long—the day after it opened, the United States entered World War I. However, the production was a milestone because it was the first time black artists appeared on Broadway in serious dramatic roles, showing complex human emotions and yearnings. It was viewed by the African American community as a resounding rejection of the trivial humor and stereotypes perpetuated by historic minstrel shows.

From Con Artist to Emperor

It took three years for another drama with an African American cast to appear on Broadway. *The Emperor Jones*, written by white playwright Eugene O'Neill, is the story of Brutus Jones, a convicted black murderer who escapes from prison to an unnamed island in the Caribbean where he uses his skills as a con artist to become emperor.

The Emperor Jones starred Charles Gilpin in the important title role. However, Jones speaks a crude black southern dialect, and his character perpetuates a stereotypical view of the African American male as a swindler, huckster, and dangerous criminal. Commenting on this aspect of the play, the *Boston Globe* praised Gilpin, writing that "only an actor of genuine power could save some of [the scenes] from becoming ludicrous."[55] For his part, Gilpin often changed the dialogue—much to O'Neill's displeasure—using terms such as black baby, Negro, or colored man in place of offensive racial slurs.

Despite the criticism, *The Emperor Jones* was an overnight success after its November 1, 1920, premiere in the Provincetown Theatre. Thousands of people wanted tickets, and lines reached around the block. As a result, the production was moved to a larger theater on Broadway and extra shows were added. For his role in the play, Gilpin was awarded the NAACP Spingarn Medal for the highest achievement of a black American.

While racial stereotypes were largely overlooked in *The Emperor Jones*, O'Neill's next play, *All God's Chillun Got Wings*, was offensive to white audiences. Starring black actor Paul Robeson and white actress Mary Blair, *All God's Chillun* was about interracial marriage and called for Blair to kiss Robeson's hand onstage. When the press was notified of this provocative storyline, many newspaper editorial boards demanded the play be banned. This inflamed the public, and the cast was flooded with death threats. Although there was fear that riots would break out or the theater would be bombed, the debate only fueled demand for tickets. *All God's Chillun* opened peacefully in November 1924, and Robeson and Blair were catapulted to international stardom.

Spread of Plays and Musicals

By the time *All God's Chillun* premiered, *Shuffle Along* was being performed by road companies in packed theaters across the United States. The

The Emperor Jones *was the first real hit for the Provincetown Theater, and the box office was flooded with ticket requests. Paul Robeson is shown here in the film version of the play.*

A Stereotypical Image

When all-black casts began appearing in Broadway plays in the early 1920s, it was viewed as a major accomplishment. However, judged by today's standards, the plays might be seen as racially insensitive, if not blatantly offensive. For example, in *Shuffle Along*, several of the characters are swindlers, who only view light-skinned black women as desirable. Even a serious play such as *The Emperor Jones* perpetuated the stereotypical image of the uncivilized, uneducated southern black man. In the play, character Brutus Jones describes his life of crime:

> *Maybe I goes to jail dere for gettin' in an argument wid razors ovah a crap game. Maybe I gits twenty years when dat colored man die. Maybe I gits in 'nother argument wid de prison guard was overseer ovah us when we're wukin' de roads. Maybe he hits me wid a whip and I splits his head wid a shovel and runs away and files de chain off my leg and gits away safe. Maybe I does all dat an' maybe I don't. It's a story I tells you so's you knows I'se de kind of man dat if you evah repeats one words of it, I ends yo' stealin' on dis yearth mighty ... quick!*[1]

1. Eugene O'Neill, *The Emperor Jones: Scene One*, Eoneill.com, accessed February 16, 2018. www.eoneill.com/texts/jones/i.htm.

play "legitimized the black musical, [spawned] dozens of imitators, [and made African American musicals] a Broadway staple,"[56] according to theater historian Allen Woll.

Despite the success of *Shuffle Along*, the play was almost doomed before it started. No black musical comedy had opened on Broadway since 1910, and those that premiered in earlier times had failed. As Walton explained in 1924, white promoters would not produce black revues because, "white amusement seekers would not patronize a colored show as a legitimate theatrical proposition. Negro entertainment [was regarded] merely as a lure for slumming parties [only suitable on] the fringe of the theatre district."[57]

The creators of *Shuffle Along* overcame these difficulties through sheer talent. Performers Flournoy Miller and Aubrey Lyles were known for their hilarious comedy routines on the vaudeville circuit. (Vaudeville was a type of popular entertainment featuring singing, dancing, and comedy acts.) Writers Noble Sissle and Eubie Blake, known as the Dixie Duo, were also established vaudeville stars. Blake, the most famous of the crew, began playing the organ when he was five years old, composed "Charleston Rag" on the piano when he was 12, and was playing keyboards with Big Jim Europe's jazz band at 18. Blake had written most of the music for *Shuffle Along* with Sissle long before the play premiered. However, the Dixie Duo could not get white producers to buy their songs and publish them as sheet music, which was the primary way to make money in the early 20th century.

In 1920, the creators of *Shuffle Along* were struggling to produce a play that was conceived primarily for black audiences on Broadway, the most competitive entertainment environment in the world. With no outside financing, they were forced to pay for rehearsals with their vaudeville salaries. Many of the actors, singers, and dancers worked for free, hoping for a payday when the show began playing.

Shuffle Along opened first in Washington, D.C., in early 1921. After two successful weeks and a short run in Philadelphia, Pennsylvania, the producers were able to take it to New York. Amazed that the show went on despite their shoestring budget, Blake later remarked,

I still don't know how we did it. We didn't have money for nothin'—not for train fare when we needed it, not for scenery. It just seemed that we found everything just when we needed it. I believe if something is meant to happen, it's going to happen. That's how we all felt! It was like watchin' new miracles every day.[58]

The money shortage also meant that Blake and the others could not hire big-name stars. However, after the success of *Shuffle Along*, several of the singers and dancers found stardom. Josephine Baker became famous on Broadway and an international sensation nearly overnight after she appeared in the show's chorus line. Florence Mills, a cabaret singer and comic, was soon the top black star in America and went on to perform to critical acclaim in London, Paris, and other European cities. Sheet music and records of songs from the revue also became worldwide hits, including "I'm Just Wild About Harry," "Bandana Days," "Love Will Find a Way," and "In Honeysuckle Time."

Blake also became a major star. During intermission on opening night, white audience members were so awed by him that they approached him just to touch his hand or coat sleeve. Commenting on this reaction, Blake stated, "Well you got to feel that. It made me feel like, well, at last, I'm a human being."[59]

After the success of *Shuffle Along*, Sissle and Blake wrote other popular musicals, including *Chocolate Dan-*

An International Sensation

Josephine Baker became an international star nearly overnight after first appearing in the chorus line of *Shuffle Along* at the age of 17. Baker, however, was not hired for her stunning beauty. Instead, she impressed the show's musical producer, Eubie Blake, with her comedic dance performances, mugging, crossing her eyes, making faces, tripping, falling out of step with the other dancers, and humorously rushing to catch up. When she appeared before audiences, she quickly stole the show and was soon one of the most popular and well-paid members of the cast.

After a triumphant run in *Shuffle Along*, Baker appeared in *Chocolate Dandies*, but she could not endure American racism. In 1925, she fled Harlem and embarked on an extremely successful career in Paris. Her dance routines highlighted seemingly impossible contorted dances patterned on the movements of African animals. Author Phyllis Rose described Baker's dancing: "She splayed her arms and legs as if they were dislocated. She shook and shimmied constantly, moving like a snake … Finally she left the stage on all fours, legs stiff, rear end in the air, higher than her head, looking as awkward as a young giraffe."[1] When not imitating animals, Baker created near riots parading down Paris streets with a pet leopard on a leash.

During World War II and the German occupation of France, Baker was a member of the French Resistance and worked with the Red Cross. After her 1956

dies, which featured Baker. Blake also did solo projects, such as the musical *Blackbirds of 1928*, featuring Mills, Ethel Waters, dancer Bill "Bojangles" Robinson, and international hit songs such as "Diga Diga Doo," and "I Can't Give You Anything But Love." Other popular black revues that played Broadway in the wake of *Shuffle Along* included *Rang Tang*, *Keep Shufflin'*, and the Fats Waller production *Hot Chocolates*.

Accurate Depictions

African American comedy revues were beloved by black and white audiences. However, some of the intellectuals behind the New Negro renaissance were appalled upon seeing African American comedians performing in heavy blackface makeup on Broadway. Despite the criticism of the literati crowd, successful African American revues paved the way for a second wave of dramatic plays with black casts. Some of these shows,

retirement, she continued to perform occasionally until her death in 1975.

1. Quoted in Cary D. Wintz, ed., *Harlem Speaks: A Living History of the Harlem Renaissance*. Naperville, IL: Sourcebooks, 2007, p. 314.

Josephine Baker refused to perform in front of segregated audiences. At 31, she moved to Europe and became a French citizen.

written mostly by white playwrights, were credited with accurately depicting black life in the United States.

Black Experience Portrayed in the Theater

In 1926, Paul Green's *In Abraham's Bosom* opened at the Provincetown Theatre. The Pulitzer Prize-winning play portrays a black farmer who struggles against society to obtain an education. In the end, he kills his white half-brother and is hanged by a mob. Green grew up on a cotton farm in North Carolina, and according to newspaper editor Roy Parker Jr., the play is based on "the shame and outrage that he felt for the atrocities … of the chain gang, and of the discrimination that race and poverty visited on common people."[60]

DuBose Heyward was another white author from the Carolinas who had viewed the plight of southern black Americans through sympathetic eyes.

His 1925 novel, *Porgy*, tells the story of a disabled homeless man living in the fictitious Catfish Row area of Charleston, South Carolina. The year after it was published, Heyward's wife, Dorothy, an Ohio-born playwright, began adapting it for the stage. The play premiered at the Guild Theatre on Broadway on October 10, 1927. According to Hughes and Meltzer, *Porgy* "featured a cast composed of the finest Negro actors ever assembled in one production up to that time."[61]

Whatever the talents of its cast, *Porgy* was not within reach of most Harlem residents. The tickets were $25 each (a week's pay for an average Harlem resident), and moreover, the Guild was a segregated theater. So while Harlem's richest citizens were able to afford a

Porgy's story is one of the few in entertainment history that was adapted as a play and opera. It was also turned into a film with Sidney Poitier, a still of which is shown here.

ticket to *Porgy*, they were forced to sit in the "colored section" in the balcony. Nevertheless, as historian David Levering Lewis wrote in *When Harlem Was in Vogue*, "Everybody in Harlem seemed to know someone in the cast … [and] 'Porgy' was Harlem's play."[62] Cast members, such as Rose McClendon, who played Serena; Frank Wilson, who played Porgy; Evelyn Ellis, who played Bess; and Percy Verwayne, who played Sportin' Life, were well-known bohemians who hung around the Harlem club called Dark Tower. In addition, the street corners and storefront churches on *Porgy*'s Catfish Row were based on director Rouben Mamoulian's tours through Harlem. Since many residents of the neighborhood had read the book, Lewis noted, "Harlemites knew the lines of the play almost as well as the understudies did."[63]

Porgy ran for 850 performances and was considered one of the greatest dramas of the Harlem Renaissance. It was remade in 1935 into the opera *Porgy and Bess*, with music by George Gershwin and lyrics by Ira Gershwin and Dorothy Heyward. *Porgy and Bess* was revived again in 1959 by MGM for a film version featuring an all-star African American cast, including Sidney Poitier, Dorothy Dandridge, Sammy Davis Jr., Pearl Bailey, and Diahann Carroll.

Before starring in *Porgy*, Frank Wilson was a Harlem mailman who wrote plays in his spare time. After becoming a Broadway star, Wilson used his connections to produce a play he had written called *Meek Mose*. According to Lewis, the play, which opened February 6, 1928, "provided employment for every professional Afro-American actor [in Harlem] and a few relatives besides."[64] Harlem residents were also proud that New York mayor Jimmy Walker addressed the crowd on opening night at the Princess Theater. Moreover, other politicians and members of the city's upper classes were in attendance. However, some people were upset by the stereotypes in the play, and the majority of critics were not impressed.

Meek Mose closed in less than a month. By this time, a series of events had begun shaking the foundations of African American theater on Broadway. In November 1927, Florence Mills died unexpectedly from acute appendicitis at the height of her fame. Meanwhile, Harlem Renaissance promoters Alain Locke, James Weldon Johnson, and W. E. B. Du Bois had moved on to new interests and were paying less attention to black theater and drama. More devastating, a new technology created irresistible competition for Broadway: movies. In 1927, silent movies came to an end when films began including sound. These "talkies" drew audiences, actors, and writers away from live

Simple and Profound

In his book *Black Manhattan*, James Weldon Johnson highly praised the cast of *The Green Pastures* and its creator Marc Connelly:

> *[In previous dramas, the] Negro removed any lingering doubts as to his ability to do intelligent acting. In "The Green Pastures," he established conclusively his capacity to get the utmost subtleties across the footlights, to convey the most delicate nuances of emotion, to create the atmosphere in which the seemingly unreal becomes for the audience the most real thing in life. "The Green Pastures" is a play so simple and yet so profound, so close to the earth and yet so spiritual, that it is as high a test for those powers in the actor as any play the American stage has seen—a higher test than many of the immortalized classics ... The acting in "The Green Pastures" seems so spontaneous and natural that one is tempted to believe the players are not really acting. In the light of the truth about the matter, this is a high compliment ... What Mr. Connelly actually did was to work something very little short of a miracle. No one seems able to remember any playwright, play, and company of players that have together received such unanimous praise as these ... in the making of "The Green Pastures".[1]*

1. James Weldon Johnson, *Black Manhattan*. New York, NY: Da Capo, 1991, pp. 218–219.

theater, and attendance fell dramatically. Then, in October 1929, a massive stock market crash signaled the beginning of the Great Depression. Four months later, *The Green Pastures* opened at the Mansfield Theater.

The Green Pastures, written by white author Marc Connelly, focused on African American tales of spirituality based on Bible stories and biblical figures. Featuring black angels, choirs, and a character called De Lawd (the Lord),

Connelly described his work as "an attempt to present certain aspects of a living religion in the terms of its believers. The religion is that of thousands of Negroes in the deep South."[65]

The play was universally praised. With songs performed by the Hall Johnson Choir and Richard B. Harrison playing De Lawd, *The Green Pastures* ran for 557 sold-out performances. The play was then taken on extensive tours in both the North and South before returning to Broadway for a five-year run.

Fade to Black

The Green Pastures was the last great African American drama of the Harlem Renaissance. By the time it debuted, the United States was in the grip of an unprecedented economic disaster. Many of New York's millionaires lost everything, while more than one-third of American adults were unemployed. In this stressed economy, black Americans were the first to be fired. The trend affected Broadway producers and entertainers as well. Although *Shuffle Along* had made an astounding $8 million, when Eubie Blake tried to revive the show in 1933, the revue closed after only two weeks. Blake said,

"We saw it wasn't going anywhere … It wasn't the show, it was the times … So we went on the road. We really worked. We gave it all we had. But it was no use. We got to L.A. and didn't even have enough money left to get us home."[66]

It was President Franklin D. Roosevelt's federal New Deal program, the Works Progress Administration (WPA), that helped Blake. Designed to help the unemployed, the WPA gave a number of grants to artists, writers, and entertainers. Blake was one of them. He wrote musicals for the government—but he was lucky. Many of Harlem's residents were not so fortunate. The stage lights dimmed, the audiences stayed home—and the Harlem Renaissance faded to black.

Chapter Five

EXPERIENCE AS ART

For two decades, residents of Harlem used their talents to write engaging stories and poems, sing and play passionate songs with profound lyrics, and perform powerful roles on stage to let the world see how they perceived the experience of being black. They fought people's racism and stereotyping at the same time as they entertained and amused them. Another group of people were also exploring their African American heritage and sharing it with others: the artists of the Harlem Renaissance. Ironically enough, in order to express their American experiences, many of them had to learn how to imitate Europeans. Some of the most successful black artists of the 20th century worked and studied in France to further their art careers.

Sculptor Meta Vaux Warrick Fuller was one such artist. She moved to Paris in 1899 to study sculpture at the Académie Colarossi and drawing at the École des Beaux-Arts (School of Fine Arts). Although she was only 22 at the time, Fuller's work was admired by famed French artist Auguste Rodin whose statue *The Thinker* is one of the most famous sculptures in the world. With Rodin's encouragement, Fuller entered the prestigious Paris art exhibition known as the Salon d'Automne in 1903. The Salon d'Automne, attended by some of the world's most influential artists and art buyers, is known for its famously tough judges, but Fuller's masterpiece *The Wretched* was accepted for the show.

The French judges doubtlessly appreciated the emotional impact of *The Wretched*. Each of the seven figures in the sculpture represents a form of human misery. They include a deformed child, an old man sickened by hunger, a woman who had lost her loved ones, and a woman driven insane by sorrow.

After moving back to the United States,

In 1910, a fire destroyed most of the paintings and sculptures Meta Vaux Warrick Fuller had created. She was so devastated that she stopped producing art. Her work The Wretched *is shown here.*

Fuller married a Liberian physician and moved to Framingham, Massachusetts, in 1909. Against the strong disapproval of her husband, Fuller single-handedly built her own sculpture studio. Within its walls, she explored what historian Benjamin Brawley calls "the tragedy of the Negro race."[67]

Fuller's artwork was inspired by the Pan-African philosophy of W. E. B. Du Bois, whom she met in Paris in 1900. Pan-Africanism connected black Americans with their African legacy and led Fuller to create the sculpture *Ethiopia Awakening* in 1914. This bronze sculpture symbolizes the emergence of the New Negro from her African roots. Her legs and lower torso are wrapped like a mummy, but a beautiful black woman with long flowing hair and the headdress of an Egyptian queen emerges from the binding. The symbolism of the sculpture is explored by curator David Driskell and his coauthors in their book *Harlem Renaissance: Art of Black America*. They wrote,

> Ethiopia Awakening *was a truly Pan-Africanist work of art. Fuller's art [demonstrated the] … union between Black Africa and Black America … The symbol of Africa who reaches forth from bondage to freedom connotes the awakening of the forces of good, truth, and beauty in rebellion against … [the white] exploitation of African peoples and resources.*[68]

As a black female artist working during an era of excessive racism and sexism, Fuller keenly understood the concept of breaking free from restraints. This theme was clearly displayed in the 1919 sculpture *Mary Turner (Silent Protest Against Mob Violence)*. However, unlike *Ethiopia Awakening*, this statue was based on horrific events.

In 1918, pregnant Mary Turner was accused of plotting to kill a white man, aided by her husband and two other black men in Valdosta, Georgia. Although the accusations were false, Turner and the three men were lynched, burned, and riddled with bullets. In the aftermath, thousands of African Americans marched in a silent protest down Fifth Avenue in New York City. Fuller was deeply moved by the demonstration and, according to Mary Schmidt Campbell, former executive director of Harlem's Studio Museum, Fuller "memorialized the awakening defiance of her people in her sculpture … Mary Turner … a poignant portrayal of a woman struggling to define and free herself."[69]

Although Fuller never lived in Harlem, her work inspired Manhattan-based artist Augusta Savage, another female sculptor who struggled against chauvinism (excessive loyalty to one's own gender) and bigotry (intolerance toward someone who is different). Beyond the art world, many writers, musicians, and dancers of the 1920s admired Fuller's spirit and style, which symbolized the emergence of the New Negro. She continued to create profoundly beautiful works until her death in 1962.

The Role of African Americans in the Modern World

Like Fuller, painter Aaron Douglas worked with a European artist and was strongly influenced by the design elements of African art and African American imagery. Douglas embarked on a successful painting career after moving from Topeka, Kansas, to Harlem in 1925 at the age of 26. In New York, his drawings greatly impressed German painter and designer Winold Reiss, who gave Douglas a full scholarship to his art school. Reiss encouraged Douglas to turn away from the European art traditions he learned in school and urged him to "express

A Reflection of Heritage

Sculptor Augusta Savage was a renowned artist and educator who was born in 1892 in Florida. From an early age, she realized that she wanted to become a sculptor, but her Methodist minister father disagreed because he believed art was pagan. Frustrated that she could not practice her art, when she was an adult, Savage moved to New York. When she arrived in Harlem, she worked as a teacher and an artist. Her sculptures reflected African American culture and emphasized black facial features. Her sculpture, *The Harp*, for example, was influenced by Negro spirituals and hymns. In 1932, Savage established the Savage Studio of Arts and Crafts in Harlem to teach adults about art. Five years later, she became the first director of the Harlem Community Art Center, an institution funded by the WPA. Here, African Americans could learn about their culture through the study of fine arts.

racial commitment to his art."[70] Douglas did so, exploring issues of race, slavery, and the role of black Americans in the modern world.

Douglas's work cleverly combines several art styles that were extremely popular. He drew on the influences of art deco, a style characterized by geometric forms, sweeping curves, and models with elongated torsos. Douglas was also inspired by cubism and the art nouveau genre, which used elements found in nature, such as vines, leaves, flowers, birds, and the human form. Describing his style, Douglas stated,

I wanted to create something new and modern that fitted in with Art Deco and the other things that were taking the country by storm. That is how I came upon the notion to use a number of things such as Cubism and a style with straight lines to emphasize the mathematical relationship of things.[71]

Many of Douglas's angular, stylized figures are presented as silhouettes. The figures are painted with bodies forward but faces in profile. However, the single eye is drawn as if viewed from the front, not the side. This style is seen in ancient Egyptian art and referred to as the Egyptian form by Douglas.

The Success of Aaron Douglas

Shortly after his arrival in Harlem, Douglas met Du Bois, who hired him to work in the mailroom at *Crisis*. Within weeks, however, Douglas was drawing

The simplicity of style and color in Aaron Douglas's paintings emphasized the message he wanted to convey. Shown here is Aspects of Negro Life: From Slavery to Reconstruction.

illustrations for articles in the NAACP newspaper. After seeing the quality of his work, Alain Locke commissioned Douglas to create illustrations for *The New Negro*, a book that played a central role in the Harlem Renaissance. Soon after, Charles S. Johnson, who had originally encouraged Douglas to move to New York, began using the artist's work in *Opportunity*.

With the three founding fathers of the renaissance acting as mentors and patrons, Douglas quickly recognized that he was about to become a major success. He began to vocalize the Pan-African views of black cultural superiority. In late

1925, in a letter to his future wife, Alta Sawyer, he wrote,

At my present rate of progress, I'll be a giant in two years, I want to be frightful to look at. A veritable black terror. They (White America) believe that a black artist is impossible. They have good grounds for their belief. Most of us are utterly despicable. Most of us feel that we have reached the heights when we have depicted their chalky faces and disgusting sentimentality or filled yards of canvas with feeble imitations of their second rate "little masters."[72]

Douglas's attitudes endeared him to Harlem's literati. Before long, he moved in with Zora Neale Hurston and Wallace Thurman. He also became friends with Langston Hughes and began illustrating his poems on the pages of *Fire!!* After moving out of the manor,

Four Differing Aspects

When Aaron Douglas painted the four-panel series *Aspects of Negro Life* at the New York Public Library in Harlem, he wanted to depict a Pan-African message and connect black American culture to Africa while educating the viewer about black history.

The first panel, *The Negro in an African Setting*, depicts the action of a silhouetted couple dancing in a tribal circle. This emphasizes the importance of dance and music in black culture. This joyous scene is followed by *Into Bondage*, depicting proud Africans in chains glumly walking to slave ships as a beam of light shines down on one figure who looks to the sky.

The most intricate panel, *From Slavery to Reconstruction*, shows slaves picking cotton on the left side, while a trumpet player and dancer perform on the right. The slaves are tormented by Klansmen on horses painted in tones of red, orange, and brown. A black politician is making a speech in the center of the painting, while Civil War soldiers march in the background. As is typical in Douglas's work, buildings, such as a factory and the U.S. Capitol, are painted as majestic but unattainable.

The final panel, *Song of the Towers*, presents a saxophone player as an icon of jazz music. This figure represents the melding of African heritage, African American culture, and black national identity. Like the other panels of the series, it is painted with Douglas's trademark shadings of concentric circles and angular beams of light.

Douglas rented his own apartment, which became the center of social activity for the writers, artists, dancers, musicians, poets, and playwrights of the New Negro movement.

Despite his lively social life, Douglas worked tirelessly to create permanent images during the Harlem Renaissance. In addition to his newspaper and magazine work, he illustrated book covers for James Weldon Johnson's *The Autobiography of an Ex-Colored Man*, Thurman's *The Blacker the Berry*, and Claude McKay's *Home to Harlem*. These designs feature Douglas's unique flat, silhouetted figures, the lines drawn in such a way as to give a sense of movement to the characters.

The sharp contrasting colors of Douglas's book cover illustrations were softened considerably in a series of paintings that he created at the request of James

Weldon Johnson for his book of poems *God's Trombones: Seven Negro Sermons in Verse*. The book was inspired by Bible stories, black spirituals, recent African American history, and black American culture. The paintings, including *Noah's Ark*, *Study for God's Trombones*, and *The Crucifixion*, are executed in monochromatic tones. For example, *God's Trombones*, which depicts a silhouette of a black man standing among jungle foliage and struggling with chains, is created in tones of light and dark blue. *The Crucifixion*, with a black man struggling under the weight of a giant cross, is done in various tones of purple. Painted in the style of cubism and the forms of African sculpture, these canvases showed Douglas as a pioneering artist who invented his own painting genre.

The Jazz Age

The paintings for *God's Trombones* sparked an increased demand for Douglas's work. While he continued to illustrate for publications, in 1927, he painted a mural for the new Club Ebony in Harlem. It was his first large-scale public work. Unveiled when the club opened, the mural was filled with Pan-African cultural symbols in contrast with nature and the modern world. These characteristic elements of a Douglas painting were described in a 1927 article in the newspaper the *Kansas City Call*:

> There are tropical settings of huge trees and flowers, figures of African tom-tom players and dancers, pictures of the American Negro with a banjo and in cakewalk [dance]. On the main panel silhouetted against a background of modern skyscrapers are the forms of contemporary race dancers and musicians.[73]

The mural was a visual history of black music, and some of the so-called race dancers and musicians painted beneath the skyscrapers were in attendance on opening night. Florence Mills, just back from a whirlwind European tour, was the guest of honor. Other luminaries included Mac Rae and his Ten Ebony Stompers, Ethel Waters, Paul Robeson, W. E. B. Du Bois, and Wallace Thurman. According to one reporter, Douglas's mural created a

> true Jazz Age atmosphere [and the] elite of Harlem … kept the swank new club packed until five in the morning. Gorgeous gowns, furs, shawls, and jewels vied with the elegance of thick velvet carpets and sunken damask upholstery while surrounding all were the startling blues, reds, yellows, and blacks of Aaron Douglas's painted jungle and jazzboes [jazz musicians].[74]

The 1929 stock market crash put an end to such glittering Harlem scenes, but Douglas managed to thrive. While many of Harlem's performers, artists, and authors struggled, Douglas produced seven murals in seven years, from 1930 to 1937. Critics consider these public paintings to be among the artist's best. Some

The Renaissance on Film

Some of the people in the Harlem Renaissance captured the period on film instead of canvas. James Van Der Zee was a photographer who depicted African Americans in poses showing self-respect, style, and optimism.

Couple Wearing Raccoon Coats is one of Van Der Zee's most famous pictures and one that encapsulates the era. The photograph of a man and a woman posed with their expensive automobile presents a picture of black upper-class life rarely seen in the United States at that time. This was among many of Van Der Zee's photographs showing African Americans in pursuit of the American Dream at sporting events, family gatherings, funerals, weddings, and barbershops. Van Der Zee photographed black celebrities such as Marcus Garvey, heavyweight champion Jack Johnson, dancer Bill "Bojangles" Robinson, and singers Florence Mills and Mamie Smith. Working out of his studio, Guarantee Photos, on 135th Street, Van Der Zee also shot portraits of families, babies, brides, and grooms. His signature technique involved using darkroom tricks and double exposures to give his portraits an interesting edge. For example, Wedding Portrait with the Superimposed Image of a Little Girl, shows a shadowy youngster holding a doll at the feet of the bride and groom, symbolizing the predicted future of the couple.

Van Der Zee was also a dedicated musician, playing the piano with such jazz giants as Fletcher Henderson. However, he will always be remembered for his photographs that preserve the dignity, independence, and joy of the Harlem residents during the renaissance.

might never have been painted if not for the Depression.

Throughout the 1930s, President Roosevelt's New Deal programs provided WPA art grants to public institutions such as libraries and historically black colleges and universities. One such grant paid for Douglas's Aspects of Negro Life.

Douglas also painted murals at Fisk University in Nashville, Tennessee, where he took a job as assistant professor of art education in 1938. He taught painting at Fisk until his retirement in 1966 and died in Nashville in 1979. Although he spent the last half of his life in Tennessee, Douglas will always be remembered as the "pioneering Africanist [and] the father of Black American art,"[75] a title given to him by Locke.

Satire and Legend

Many African American artists created

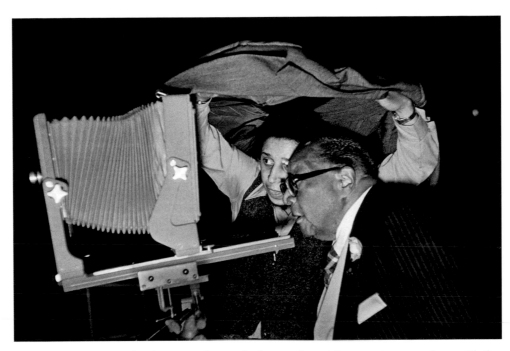

James Van Der Zee's photographs worked to end racial stereotypes and provided inspiration for other African Americans.

art based on black American life, culture, legend, and tradition. These artists were introduced to the public through exhibits sponsored by the Harmon Foundation. This prestigious organization, named for the white patron of the arts, William E. Harmon, began awarding prizes for achievement in art in 1926.

Harmon Foundation exhibitions were seen all over New York City, and these shows provided African American artists with widespread exposure to the general public. The publicity attracted black artists from across the country, and the number of artists in the foundation registry grew from about 10 in 1926 to more than 300 in 1929.

Palmer Hayden worked as a custodian to pay for art supplies. He won a Harmon Foundation Gold Award for Distinguished Achievement in Fine Arts in 1926 with the painting *Fetiche et Fleures*

(*Fetish and Flowers*). This work is a still life of an African mask, or fetish, from Gabon; a tablecloth from the Congo; and a table with a vase of flowers. Like other painters at the time, Hayden used African symbols to explore the roots of black American art.

Hayden's contributions to the Harlem Renaissance included depictions of African subjects in their humble homes, scenes from black folk stories, life in the rural South, and life in Harlem. Hayden had grown up in Wide Water, Virginia, and his childhood memories of small-town residents influenced many of his paintings.

Hayden generated great controversy with his images portraying African Americans with cartoonish, exaggerated features and grins reminiscent of blackface minstrel shows. His subjects, such as those in *Nous Quatre à Paris* (*We Four in Paris*), often had round, bald heads and large eyes, noses, ears, and lips. Art historian James A. Porter considered these paintings tasteless and said Hayden's work pandered to racist appetites for stereotypical images of black people. However, Locke defended Hayden, believing he was part of a group of young artists who were inspired by the New Negro movement "and its crusade of folk expression in all the arts."[76] Hayden explained that black people sometimes acted like minstrel clowns, wearing expressions such as those in his paintings to hide their true feelings when in the presence of white people.

In 1932, Hayden was assigned to a WPA program for the U.S. Treasury Art Project. His assignment, paying $30 a week, was to paint scenes of daily life in Harlem. One of the most enduring images from this series is 1938's *Midsummer Night in Harlem*, which shows dozens of figures sitting on stoops in front of Harlem row houses, leaning out apartment windows, or driving in cars. The dark faces and bright white teeth of the characters offended Porter who said the painting reminded him of old-time posters for minstrel shows that used to be plastered on city buildings and fences. However, Hayden considered the work satire, saying the humorous and ironic depictions were meant to mock white stereotypes.

Hayden's most renowned work consists of a series of paintings about the folk hero John Henry created between 1944 and 1954. Henry was a steel-driving man, whose ability to lay track for railroads was legendary. Henry entered into a competition with a steam-powered drill, trying to drive in more spikes and beat the machine. John Henry died with his hammer in his hand after winning the contest.

Hayden immortalized John Henry's story on 12 canvases. Commenting on the series, he said, Henry was "a powerful and popular working man who belonged to my section of the country and to my own race."[77] The critically acclaimed series helped Hayden achieve widespread respect, and in later years, his work was displayed at prestigious galleries. While many people missed the satire in Hayden's early images, they were based on the double-consciousness philosophy of Du Bois, who wrote that black Americans were continually forced to look at themselves through the eyes of their oppressors.

Natural Expression in Art

Like Hayden, artist William H. Johnson often attracted controversy. Although he was trained as a traditional academic painter at the National Academy of Design in New York, he painted in the primitive, folk, or native style. This style is based on deliberately crude images resembling the drawings of children. When a critic asked Johnson why he abandoned his training as a talented academic painter, he replied, "My aim is to express in a natural way what I feel both rhythmically and spiritually, all that has been saved up in my family of primitiveness and tradition."[78]

William H. Johnson is shown here creating one of paintings. He painted in a primitive style that allowed him to fully express himself.

Johnson used expressionism combined with an almost cartoonlike technique in brightly colored paintings such as *Chain Gang*, *Young Man in a Vest*, *Café*, and *Sis and L'il Sis*. These paintings are commentaries not only on the positive aspects of African American life, but also on the social troubles faced by black Americans.

Like many other artists of the Harlem Renaissance, Johnson received less attention and adulation than the authors, singers, musicians, and dancers. However, artwork by Johnson, Douglas, Hayden, Savage, and more provide a priceless visual record of the Jazz Age and the Harlem Renaissance.

Epilogue

FROM RENAISSANCE TO RIOT

The Harlem Renaissance is remembered as a time of great creativity, when black writers, musicians, and artists helped change widespread attitudes about African Americans. As Langston Hughes described it, "some Harlemites … thought the race problem had at last been solved through Art… They were sure the New Negro would lead a new life from then on in green pastures of tolerance."[79] It was true that black authors during the renaissance were published more often, and Broadway plays with all-black casts were largely successful. However, the belief that things would significantly change for the better was somewhat naive. Hughes pointed out that the "ordinary Negro hadn't heard of the Negro Renaissance. And if they had it hadn't raised their wages any."[80] With the onset of the Great Depression at the end of 1929, those already low wages fell dramatically.

In 1933, another economic disaster hit when Prohibition was repealed. The white patrons who flocked to Harlem speakeasies to buy bootleg liquor could now obtain legal drinks in their own neighborhoods. While some Harlem speakeasies converted to legitimate bars, many shut their doors, laying off untold numbers of black waiters, waitresses, busboys, cooks, bartenders, dancers, musicians, managers, and others.

By 1935, nearly half of all Harlem residents were unemployed. The high rents in Harlem had not decreased, however, and many single apartments were now occupied by two or three families. Harlem quickly turned from a great metropolis into a poverty stricken stretch of Manhattan. The hard times created an exodus among the elite of the Harlem Renaissance. Black writers and literary promoters such as Hughes, James

A riot broke out in Harlem in 1935. It was the first in New York City in the 20th century. However, it was followed by many more over the coming years.

Weldon Johnson, Charles S. Johnson, and W. E. B. Du Bois fled New York City, many relocating to Paris.

The bleak economic conditions in Harlem did not stop the migration of poor, uneducated African Americans from the South. Between 1930 and 1935, another 75,000 black migrants entered New York, most of them settling in Harlem. The poverty, hopelessness, and overcrowding created great stress and was blamed for the full-blown riot that exploded in Harlem on March 19, 1935. It began when police arrested a Puerto Rican boy for stealing a 10-cent pocketknife from a white-owned business. Rumors spread that the boy was beaten to death by police, and looting began. By the next day, 200 stores were damaged, 3 African Americans were dead, more than 100 were injured, and nearly $2 million of property was destroyed. In reality, the Puerto Rican boy had been released by police before the riot began when the shopkeeper decided not to press charges.

A Lingering Impact

Even with its violence and economic hardships, Harlem was largely invisible to most Americans throughout the Great Depression and World War II. However, the influence of the Harlem Renaissance remained strong. In the decades that followed, literature from the era inspired best-selling black authors such as Ralph Ellison and Richard Wright to explore African American life. It also served to inspire modern writers such

The battle for equality and acceptance continues today, a century after the Harlem Renaissance began.

as Toni Morrison, Alice Walker, Octavia Butler, and Maya Angelou. The outstanding jazz music of Duke Ellington, Eubie Blake, and others set a standard by which all other jazz music was measured in later years. It served to encourage modern musicians such as Herbie Hancock, Miles Davis, and Wynton Marsalis. The political aspects of the Harlem Renaissance influenced a new generation of black leaders in the 1950s and 1960s. Nation of Islam leader Malcolm X and civil rights icon Martin Luther King Jr. both credited Marcus Garvey and founders of the New Negro movement for redefining black consciousness, and the progress of the era served as a starting point from which African Americans gained a spirit of self-determination and pride. In the mid-1960s, this was expressed as Black Power and through the expression "Black is Beautiful." In more recent years, this way of asserting the importance of race and equality has been seen in global movements such as Black Lives Matter and in public figures such as professional football player Colin Kaepernick and the many people he inspired to "take a knee" during the national anthem to protest racism. It is even seen in government, where Barack Obama was the first

African American president of the United States, a position he held for two terms, from 2009 to 2017.

Although it lasted little more than a decade, the Harlem Renaissance left a lasting mark on the country's history. It inspired black Americans—and black people throughout the world—to make incredible contributions to society and culture through their skills and talents as artists, authors, musicians, actors, and leaders. The influence continues to ripple even today, a reminder that the world would be a drab and different place if the Harlem Renaissance had never happened.

Notes

Introduction:
A Great Awakening

1. Paul Laurence Dunbar, *The Sport of the Gods*. Charleston, SC: BiblioBazaar, 2007, p. 47.
2. Cary D. Wintz, *Black Culture and the Harlem Renaissance*. Houston, TX: Rice University Press, 1988, p. 3.

Chapter One:
A Changing Urban Culture

3. Leon Litwack, *Trouble in Mind: Black Southerners in the Age of Jim Crow*. New York, NY: Alfred A. Knopf, 1998, p. xiv.
4. Quoted in Jervis Anderson, *This Was Harlem*. New York, NY: Farrar, Straus and Giroux, 1982, p. 56.
5. James Weldon Johnson, "The Making of Harlem," in *The New Negro: An Interpretation*, ed. Alain Locke. New York, NY: Atheneum, 1969, p. 637.
6. Johnson, "The Making of Harlem," in *The New Negro: An Interpretation*, p. 638.
7. Quoted in Tim Brooks and Richard Keith Spottswood, *Lost Sounds: Blacks and the Birth of the Recording Industry, 1890–1919*. Chicago, IL: University of Illinois Press, 2004, p. 280.
8. Quoted in Theodore G. Vincent, ed., *Voices of a Black Nation*. Trenton, NJ: Africa World, 1973, p. 68.
9. Quoted in Vincent, *Voices of a Black Nation*, p. 65.
10. Quoted in Vincent, *Voices of a Black Nation*, p. 69.
11. Marcus Garvey and Herbert Aptheker, et al., eds., *The Marcus Garvey and Universal Negro Improvement Association Papers, vol. 2*. Berkeley, CA: University of California Press, 1983, pp. 297–298.
12. Quoted in Garvey and Aptheker, et al., eds., *The Marcus Garvey and Universal Negro Improvement Association Papers*, p. 493.
13. William Edward Burghardt Du Bois and David L. Lewis, *W. E. B. Du Bois: A Reader*. New York, NY: Macmillan, 1995, p. 333.
14. Quoted in Vincent, *Voices of a Black Nation*, p. 96.
15. Quoted in Theodore Kornweibel Jr., *Seeing Red: Federal Campaigns Against Black Militancy, 1919–1925*. Bloomington, IN: Indiana University Press, 1998, p. 102.

Chapter Two:
The Written Words
of the Renaissance

16. Justin Conn, "Robertson Charter School Class Brings Harlem Renaissance to Decatur Museum," *Herald and Review*, June

19, 2017. herald-review.com/ news/local/education/robertson-charter-school-class-brings-harlem-renaissance-to-decatur-museum/article_459ab937-8f4a-56b2-b9e9-a7211580e786. html.

17. W. E. B. Du Bois, *The Souls of Black Folk*. Chicago, IL: McClurg, 1903. www.bartleby.com/114/1.html.

18. Langston Hughes, *The Fight for Freedom: The Story of the NAACP*. New York, NY: Norton, 1962, p. 203.

19. James Weldon Johnson, *Along This Way: The Autobiography of James Weldon Johnson*. New York, NY: Viking, 1933, p. 203.

20. Quoted in Wayne F. Cooper, *Claude McKay: Rebel Sojourner in the Harlem Renaissance*. Baton Rouge, LA: Louisiana State University Press, 1987, p. 68.

21. Claude McKay, *Harlem Shadows*: *The Poems of Claude McKay*. New York, NY: Harcourt Brace, 1922.

22. Quoted in Cooper, *Claude McKay*, p. 164.

23. James Weldon Johnson, ed., *The Book of American Negro Poetry*. New York, NY: Harcourt Brace, 1922. www.bartleby.com/269/1000.html.

24. Quoted in Cary D. Wintz, ed., *Harlem Speaks: A Living History of the Harlem Renaissance*. Naperville, IL: Sourcebooks, 2007, p. 354.

25. Langston Hughes, "The Weary Blues," New York, NY: Alfred A. Knopf, 1926. cai.ucdavis.edu/uccp/ workingweary.html.

26. Langston Hughes, *The Big Sea*. New York, NY: Hill and Wang, 1993, pp. 266–267.

27. Quoted in Hughes, *The Big Sea*, p. 266.

28. Hughes, *The Big Sea*, p. 267.

29. Quoted in Arna Bontemps, ed., *The Harlem Renaissance Remembered*. New York, NY: Dodd, Mead, 1972, pp. 64–65.

30. Jessie Redmon Fauset, *The Chinaberry Tree: A Novel of American Life*. New York, NY: Dover Publications, 2013, p. ix.

31. Quoted in David Levering Lewis, *When Harlem Was in Vogue*. New York, NY: Alfred A. Knopf, 1981, p. 124.

32. Quoted in Lewis, *When Harlem Was in Vogue*, p. 125.

33. Alain Locke, ed., *The New Negro*. New York, NY: Atheneum, 1969, p. xvii.

34. Quoted in Steven Watson, *The Harlem Renaissance*. New York, NY: Pantheon, 1995, p. 89.

35. Hughes, *The Big Sea*, p. 235.

36. Quoted in Wintz, *Black Culture and the Harlem Renaissance*, p. 83.

37. Quoted in Hughes, *The Big Sea*, p. 235.

38. Justina Ireland, "Welcome to FIYAH," *FIYAH*, September 1, 2016. www. fiyahlitmag.com/2016/09/01/ welcome-to-fiyah.

Chapter Three: Stridin' and Stompin'

39. Quoted in Samuel A. Floyd Jr., ed., *Black Music in the Harlem Renaissance*. New York, NY: Greenwood, 1990, p. 2.

40. Hughes, *The Big Sea*, pp. 224–225.
41. Hughes, *The Big Sea*, p. 225.
42. Mark C. Gridley, *Jazz Styles: History and Analysis*. Englewood Cliffs, NJ: Prentice Hall, 1988, p. 66.
43. Quoted in Alyn Shipton, *A New History of Jazz*. New York, NY: Continuum, 2001, p. 267.
44. Mark Tucker, "The Renaissance Education of Duke Ellington," in *Black Music in the Harlem Renaissance*, p. 111.
45. Wintz, *Harlem Speaks*, p. 36.
46. Hughes, *The Big Sea*, p. 226.
47. Langston Hughes and Milton Meltzer, *Black Magic*. Englewood Cliffs, NJ: Prentice Hall, 1967, p. 80.
48. Quoted in Wintz, *Harlem Speaks*, pp. 179–180.
49. Anderson, *This Was Harlem*, p. 309.

Chapter Four:
The Renaissance on the Stage

50. Hughes, *The Big Sea*, p. 223.
51. David Krasner, *A Beautiful Pageant*. New York, NY: Palgrave Macmillan, 2003, p. 229.
52. Hughes and Meltzer, *Black Magic*, p. 123.
53. Quoted in Krasner, *A Beautiful Pageant*, p. 230.
54. James Weldon Johnson, *Black Manhattan*. New York, NY: Da Capo, 1991, p. 170.
55. Quoted in Krasner, *A Beautiful Pageant*, p. 189.
56. Allen Woll, *Black Musical Theatre: From Coontown to Dreamgirls*. Baton Rouge, LA: Louisiana State University, 1989, p. 60.
57. Quoted in Krasner, *A Beautiful Pageant*, p. 241.
58. Quoted in Al Rose, *Eubie Blake*. New York, NY: Schirmer, 1979, p. 74.
59. Quoted in Woll, *Black Musical Theatre*, p. 65.
60. Roy Parker Jr., "Paul Green's Legacy," Paul Green Foundation, May 2003. www.ibiblio.org/paulgreen/paulgreenlegacy.html.
61. Hughes and Meltzer, *Black Magic*, p. 113.
62. Lewis, *When Harlem Was in Vogue*, p. 207.
63. Lewis, *When Harlem Was in Vogue*, p. 207.
64. Lewis, *When Harlem Was in Vogue*, p. 207.
65. Quoted in Johnson, *Black Manhattan*, p. 219.
66. Quoted in Rose, *Eubie Blake*, pp. 109–110.

Chapter Five:
Experience as Art

67. Benjamin Brawley, *Women of Achievement*. Chicago, IL: Woman's American Baptist Home Mission Society, 1919, p. 68.
68. Mary Schmidt Campbell, David Driskell, et al., *Harlem Renaissance: Art of Black America*. New York, NY: Abrams, 1987, pp. 108–109.
69. Campbell et al., *Harlem Renaissance*, p. 27.
71. Quoted in Campbell et al., *Harlem Renaissance*, p. 110.
72. Quoted in Susan Earle, ed., *Aaron*

Douglas: African American Modernist. Lawrence, KS: Spencer Museum of Art, 2007, pp. 89–90.

73. Earle, *Aaron Douglas*, p. 23.
74. Quoted in Earle, *Aaron Douglas*, p. 212.
75. Quoted in Bill Egan, *Florence Mills: Harlem Jazz Queen*. Lanham, MD: Scarecrow, 2004, p. 218.
76. Quoted in Campbell et al., *Harlem Renaissance*, p. 110.
77. Quoted in Eric Hanks, "Journey from the Crossroads: Palmer Hayden's Right Turn," *International Review of African American Art 16*, no. 1, pp. 30–42. www.mhanksgallery.com/hayart.html.
78. Quoted in Theresa A. Leininger-Miller, *New Negro Artists in Paris*. New Brunswick, NJ: Rutgers University Press, 2000, p. 97.

Epilogue: From Renaissance to Riot

79. Hughes, *The Big Sea*, p. 228.
80. Hughes, *The Big Sea*, p. 228.

For More Information

Books

Arora, Sabina. *The Great Migration and the Harlem Renaissance*. New York, NY: Britannica Educational Publishing, 2015.
Learn more about the Great Migration and how the period between the Civil War and the civil rights movement affected the African American population.

Cunningham, Meghan. *Bill "Bojangles" Robinson: Dancer*. New York, NY: Cavendish Square, 2016.
Cunningham's biography of the famous dancer Bill "Bojangles" Robinson begins with his childhood in the South and details his influence during the Harlem Renaissance and beyond.

Herringshaw, DeAnn. *The Harlem Renaissance*. North Mankato, MN: ABDO Publishing, 2012.
Explore New York City's Harlem neighborhood and learn more about its famous residents and their global influence.

Honey, Maureen. *Aphrodite's Daughters: Three Modernist Poets of the Harlem Renaissance*. New Brunswick, NJ: Rutgers University Press, 2016.
This book details the work and influence of three Harlem Renaissance poets: Angelina Weld Grimké, Gwendolyn B. Bennett, and Mae V. Cowdery.

Websites

Drop Me Off in Harlem

*artsedge.kennedy-center.org/
interactives/harlem*
This website features many of
the famous faces of the Harlem
Renaissance, including visual artists,
authors, activists, and musicians.

Famous Harlem Renaissance Artists

*biography.com/people/groups/
famous-harlem-renaissance-artists*
Read the biographies of Harlem
Renaissance visual and performing
artists, including photographer James
Van Der Zee and trumpet player
Louis Armstrong.

Great Migration

*history.com/topics/black-history/
great-migration*
Learn more about the causes and
effects of the Great Migration, the
period in the early 20th century when
black Americans relocated from
southern states to large cities in the
North, including New York City.

"See Striking Photos of Harlem Street Life in the 1930s"

*time.com/4206723/photos-harlem-
street-life-1930s*
From children playing to bustling
businesses, view photos on this
website taken in New York City's
Harlem in the 1930s.

Index

Picture Credits

Cover JP Jazz Archive/Redferns/Getty Images; pp. 4–5, 7 (bottom left), 14, 23, 43, 65 Bettmann/Bettmann/Getty Images; pp. 6 (top), 28, 34, 55 Courtesy of the Library of Congress; pp. 7 (top left), 50, 78–79 Courtesy of The New York Public Library Digital Collections; p. 7 (top right) Charles Peterson/Hulton Archive/Getty Images; pp. 7 (bottom right), 85 US National Archives bot/Wikimedia Commons; p. 9 Universal History Archive/Getty Images; pp. 10, 18–19 George Rinhart/Corbis via Getty Images; p. 13 Maxger/Shutterstock.com; p. 16 Karen Huang/Rosen Publishing; p. 30 © CORBIS/Corbis via Getty Images; p. 38 PhotoQuest/Getty Images; p. 40 Everett Collection Historical/Alamy Stock Photo; pp. 44–45 Chicago History Museum/Getty Images; p. 47 The Cotton Club in Harlem, New York, in 1938 (b/w photo)/Bridgeman Images; pp. 52–53 Duke Ellington and the Cotton Club Orchestra (b/w photo)/Private Collection/Bridgeman Images; p. 58 Couple dancing at Savoy Ballroom, Harlem, 1947 (b/w photo)/Bridgeman Images; p. 61 Rob Kim/Getty Images; pp. 62–63 John Springer Collection/CORBIS/Corbis via Getty Images; p. 69 Fox Photos/Getty Images; pp. 70–71 Gjon Mili/The LIFE Picture Collection/Getty Images; p. 75 Gift of Alma de Bretteville Spreckels; p. 83 George Gardner/The Image Works; pp. 88–89 Dick Lewis/NY Daily News Archive via Getty Images; pp. 90–91 a katz/Shutterstock.com.

About the Author

Tamra Orr is the author of more than 500 educational books for readers of all ages. She lives in the Pacific Northwest with her husband and children and spends her limited free time reading, writing letters to people all over the world, and tent camping in many of Oregon's most beautiful spots. Orr graduated from Ball State University with a degree in English and Secondary Education. She has dedicated her life to writing books that will help readers understand a variety of important topics and then, hopefully, spill over into making the world a better place.